THE Gospel VS. LEGALISM

MARVIN MOORE

THE Gospel vs. LEGALISM

HOW TO DEAL WITH LEGALISM'S INSIDIOUS INFLUENCE

REVIEW AND HERALD ® PUBLISHING ASSOCIATION
HAGERSTOWN, MARYLAND 21740

The author assumes full responsibility for the accuracy of all facts and quotations as cited in this book.

Unless otherwise indicated, all Bible passages are from the Holy Bible, New International Version. Copyright © 1973, 1978, 1984, International Bible Society. Used by permission of Zondervan Bible Publishers.

This book was
Edited by Richard W. Coffen
Designed by Ron J. Pride
Typeset: 11/12 Garamond

PRINTED IN U.S.A.

99 98 97 96 95 94   10 9 8 7 6 5 4 3 2 1

Library of Congress Cataloging in Publication Data
Moore, Marvin, 1937-
    The Gospel vs. legalism : how to deal with legalism's insidious
influence / Marvin Moore.
        p.   cm.

    1. Bible. N.T. Galatians—Criticism, interpretation, etc.
2. Law and gospel—History of doctrines. 3. Seventh-day Adventists—
Doctrines. 4. Adventists—Doctrines. 5. Sabbatarians—Doctrines.
I. Title. II. Title: Gospel versus legalism.
BS2685.2.M66   1994
227'.406—dc20   93-45399
                                  CIP

ISBN 0-8280-0734-9

CONTENTS

CHAPTER 1

Getting Into Galatians—
An Introduction

I walked out of the house a frustrated preacher—not my house, but the house of a man who had invited me to talk about the Bible. When he phoned and invited me over to his house, he had said he wanted to talk about the law. Specifically, he wanted to know if the Ten Commandments still applied to Christians.

After I arrived, we chatted amiably for a few minutes, and then he raised the question again: Are the Ten Commandments applicable to God's people since the cross?

I explained why I believed they were. For one thing, Paul said that "through the law we become conscious of sin," and "through the commandment sin [becomes] utterly sinful" (Rom. 3:20; 7:13). Paul also said that "the law is holy, and the commandment is holy, righteous and good" (Rom. 7:12), and James spoke of "the perfect law that gives freedom" (James 1:25).

My host became extremely agitated. "That's not true!" he exclaimed, almost yelling in my ear. "Haven't you read that Christians are released from the law?" He pointed me to Romans 7:1-3. "'The law has authority over a man only as long as he lives,'" he read from verse 1. Then he proceeded to verse 3, which changes to feminine pronouns. "'But if her husband dies, she is released from the law of marriage'" (verse 3). "Besides, we are not under law, but under grace," and he pointed me to Romans 6:14.

I flinched. But not because of the sudden gender shift.

"And look at this!" he continued triumphantly. He turned to Galatians 3 and began reading: "'What, then, was the purpose of the law? It was added because of transgressions *until the Seed to whom the promise referred had come'*"(verse 19). He spoke the last few words with special emphasis. "It says right there that the law was in effect only until the Seed came," he said. "And if you'll look at verse 16, you'll see that the Seed is Christ."

I took a deep breath, but I didn't have a chance to get a word in edgewise.

"And here's the final proof!" he exclaimed as he jabbed a finger at verse 25: "'Now that faith has come, we are no longer under the supervision of the law.'"

Frankly, I did not know how to answer. Instead I mumbled a few words and excused myself because I had another appointment. As I walked out of the house, I was determined to get to the bottom of this problem. Not that this was my first exposure to it. I had presented my standard proof texts on law to people many times. Only occasionally did anyone come back at me with the proof texts for the other side of the question. But it had happened often enough that I was painfully aware of the apparent contradiction in the New Testament, and especially in Paul's writings, about law. In the past each time someone confronted me with the problem, I had managed to explain my way out, and each time I had resolved that someday I would study the problem until I found the answer. This time I knew that "someday" had become "now."

The next day I got out my Bible and began. I decided to start with Paul's Epistle to the Galatians, since that's where most of the problems are, especially in chapter 3. However, I started with chapter 1 on the assumption that I had to understand the context of the entire book if I was to understand the problem passages in chapter 3.

After a few months of prayerful study I finally found my answer. It wasn't easy, but I found that it is possible to bring a problem to the Word and find the answers. That was in 1984. Since that time I have had opportunity to write out my views in a series of Bible study guides, and I have given a series of lectures on audiotape on the subject of the law in Galatians. Finally, I decided it was time to write a book—the book you are now reading.

I should perhaps explain to you that I did not refer to any commentaries on Galatians during my study. I did not read any of the scholarly literature on the subject. I simply studied the Bible. Also, though I have a working knowledge of Greek, for the most part I did not refer to the Greek New Testament in my study of Galatians. I used the New International Version. After several years of intensive study I finally "figured out" Galatians to my satisfaction.

In other words, I am writing from a pastoral, not a scholarly, background. I lay no claim in this book to discussing every nuance of Galatians. To do that I'd have to be a scholar, which I am not. This does not mean that I doubt the validity of my conclusions. Like most people who study carefully into a particular subject, I believe that I have reached a correct understanding of Galatians, especially the problem texts in chapters 3 and 4. However, I am aware that my conclusions may be flawed, and it seems to me that the best way to find out whether I'm right is to share my views so that others, including scholars, can criticize them.

At the risk of being misunderstood, I would like to share with you one other significant conclusion I have reached from this study. But in order to do this, I need to give you a bit of background.

As I said earlier, when I began my study of Galatians I decided to study the Bible only. However, after I finished writing the chapters on Galatians 3:19-25—the most difficult passage in Paul's entire letter—my curiosity got the best of me. Did any commentator interpret Galatians the way I did? I happened to be on the campus of Andrews University at the time, so I went to the library and browsed through the Bible commentary section. I picked up the *Word Biblical Commentary* on Galatians,[1] turned to Galatians 3:19, and began reading. I discovered that the author, Richard N. Longenecker, clearly explained the Greek text of the Bible and probed the nuances of every word and phrase. The commentary is one of the finest I have ever read.

And the further I read, the more excited I got. Dr. Longenecker interpreted Galatians 3:19-25 exactly as I had interpreted it. In verse after verse he pointed out exactly the same problems in the text that I had observed, and in almost every case he explained these problems in harmony with the conclusions I had drawn. I couldn't believe it!

I share this experience with you because I want you to know that I approached Galatians exactly the same way any layperson would. Yet my conclusions are not necessarily unique. And if I can do it, so can you.

I suspect that many Christians come to Scripture with a good bit of fear that without the background of a scholar it would be impossible for them to figure out what the Bible *really* means. I have good news for all who hold this fear. It's groundless. All you need is a good modern speech translation on which to base your study, with several others for cross-checking when you run into problems.[2] It also helps to have a reputable Bible dictionary and a good commentary or two. (Just because I chose not to refer to commentaries in my study of Galatians does not mean that commentaries are unnecessary.) With these tools, all you have to do is pay careful attention to every word. Don't try to make the words mean what you want them to mean or think they ought to mean. As much as possible, set aside your preconceived ideas and the theology you grew up with, and let the words of Scripture tell you what the Bible writer means. I guarantee you that God's Word will not lead you astray.

Before we get into Galatians, I'd like to give you a bit of background about the place and the people to whom it was written. Paul wrote Galatians to a church or group of churches in central Asia Minor. (Asia Minor was roughly what we today know as Turkey.) This region was called Galatia. Paul wrote the letter in response to a doctrinal crisis in the New Testament church that involved a false teaching which he called a "different gospel" (see Gal. 1:7-9). This false gospel was being agitated by a group of Christian Jews who may have been Pharisees before their conversion to Christianity. A number of Bible translations, including the King James Version, the New King James Version, and the *New American Standard Bible*, call this group "the sect of the Pharisees" (Acts 15:5). The Revised Standard Version and the New International Version call them "the party of the Pharisees." Modern Bible students often refer to them as "Judaizers." I have chosen to call them "the Jewish party." You will be reading a lot about this Jewish party in the rest of this book. The church in Galatia appears to have been particularly susceptible to their false teachings.

You will find it helpful, as we go through Galatians, to understand a little about the structure of the book. There is an introduction and a conclusion, of course. And the body of the book can be divided into three sections: historical, theological, and practical. The following diagram shows just where each part begins and ends:

AN OUTLINE OF GALATIANS		
Part 1	**Part 2**	**Part 3**
Historical *Galatians 1:6-2:14*	**Theological** *Galatians 2:15-4:31*	**Advice About Legalism** *Galatians 5:1-6:10*

I must warn you that Paul's line of reasoning in the Epistle to the Galatians is not easy to grasp. Peter once said that Paul's letters "contain some things that are hard to understand" (2 Peter 3:16). Galatians surely must have been at the top of his list of difficult Pauline letters! I will do my best to make the Epistle easy for you to understand, but you will get the most out of reading this book if you work at it a little harder than you do most of the books you read. I suggest that you begin by reading through Paul's entire letter to the Galatians in a modern speech translation of the Bible—preferably the New International Version, since that is the version I will use throughout most of the book. Then keep the Bible by your side, opened to Galatians, as you read this book, so that you can quickly refer to it when you come to something that seems unclear.

Many people believe that in Galatians Paul addressed a doctrinal controversy that occurred nearly 2,000 years ago and that is largely irrelevant to Christians today. The main benefit from reading Galatians, they say, is the theology about justification by faith that Paul wrote in response to the Galatian heresy. Nobody today is demanding that Christians be circumcised. Therefore, Paul's practical message was for the Galatians and other Christians of his time, not ours.

That is simply not true. It is correct, of course, that we do not have to deal with the exact form of the theological heresy that the Christians at Paul's time did. I don't know of anyone who is going around insisting that modern Christians submit to circumcision and other ceremonial laws as the Jewish party demanded. But the practical lesson from Galatians has much more to do with legalism as a wrong principle of life than it does with any specific form of legalism.

I am a Seventh-day Adventist. Because of that, I have written this book from an Adventist perspective. However, I tried to keep all Christians in mind as I wrote, because I believe that Galatians has a message for all of us.

Let me be totally frank. You're going to see a lot of dirty laundry in this book. Adventist dirty laundry. The kind that no one has yet attempted to wash.

Did you ever stick your nose in a dirty clothes hamper and take a deep breath? The result wasn't very pleasant, was it? Let me assure you that Adventist dirty clothes can get awfully smelly. In fact, I might be quite embarrassed about hanging out our dirty laundry for the world to see were it not for one thing: we've all got the stuff. There isn't a Christian denomination on the face of the earth that hasn't got plenty enough and to spare. And the reason is simple: we're all infected with the disease that causes dirty laundry—it's called sin.[3]

Furthermore, we're all tempted with legalism—the effort, somehow, even if it's in the tiniest way, to be saved by our own works or to assume that something we do changes God's attitude toward us. And all too many of us, from all denominations, yield to the temptation. Legalism is not just an Adventist problem. It's a problem that every Christian has to deal with.

And that's why I'm willing to hang out the Adventist dirty laundry for you to see. Because I know that you've got some too, whatever denomination you happen to belong to. If what you learn about cleaning up dirty laundry in this book can help you live a better life in your Christian community, then it's worth it to me and my church to let you see our dirty laundry.

In fact, I believe that the best way for any of us to learn about dirty laundry and how to clean it up is to take a close look at some specific dirty laundry. I don't think my comments would be nearly as helpful if I were to write a book about legalism in general, which discussed legalism as it is found in all churches. The best way for us all to benefit from a book about legalism is to examine it up close in a denomination with plenty of it.

And I think Adventists are well qualified to offer other Christians that look. A hundred years ago many Christian denominations had prohibitions against the use of jewelry, theater attendance, dancing, playing cards, etc. The majority of denominations have dropped these prohibitions in the years since, but a few, including Seventh-day Adventists, have not. I don't have a problem with the fact that we still have these "standards," as we call them. The problem is not with the standards, but with the way we use them.

In addition to the traditional standards I just mentioned, we Adventists have added a few of our own. We have standards on health—no alcoholic beverages, no tobacco, no tea or coffee, no unclean meats, and you'd be better off if you didn't eat any meat at all, we say. Because of our emphasis on keeping the fourth commandment, we also have maintained some rather strict rules about Sabbathkeeping—don't go to work, don't play secular games, don't work in the yard, don't clean the house, don't pay the bills, don't do business on the Sabbath, etc.

Any religious organization that teaches its members to keep standards of behavior is open to someone in the church turning those standards into legalism. And the more standards a group has, the greater the possibility for abuse. Because we have retained most of the traditional rules of 100 years ago, and because we've added a number of our own, Adventists can be, I believe, an excellent case study for anyone wanting to study legalism. That's another reason that I'm willing to be specific about Adventist legalism.

If you are a Seventh-day Adventist reader, I hope you can learn more about yourself and your own spiritual life as you read this book. If you are not a Seventh-day Adventist, I hope that you will gain a greater insight not only into Seventh-day Adventists but also into your own life and the life of your own church. Whoever you are, I hope the lessons you learn from Galatians will help you be a happier Christian.

---

[1] Richard N. Longenecker, *The Word Biblical Commentary: Galatians* (Dallas: Word Books, 1990). Dr. Longenecker is Ramsey Armitage professor of New Testament, Wycliff College, University of Toronto, Canada.

[2] I used the New International Version as the basic Bible text for my study of Galatians. The Revised Standard Version and the *New American Standard Bible* are also excellent study Bibles that I could just as well have used as basic texts. In fact, I consider the NASB to be the best for technical study, because in my opinion it comes the closest to being a word-for-word, literal translation of the Bible of any that are available today.

[3] I do not mean that legalism itself is sin. Legalism is caused by the sin problem, which infects us all. Legalism causes us to say and do many unkind things that hurt others. These unkind forms of behavior are sin. Most Christians probably behave unkindly at some time or another in their lives. In some Christians legalism is an obsessive-compulsive behavior—an addiction, if you please. For these people, judgng others and letting them know about it is a way of life. That was the problem with the Jewish party in Galatia. It is still a problem today.

[4] Some Adventists think of the Sabbath primarily in terms of the rules about what not to do. That, however, is not what the Sabbath commandment is all about. Rightly observed, the Sabbath is about spending time with God and Jesus, Christian friends, people in need, etc. However, that goes beyond the scope of this book.

CHAPTER 2

Jewish and Gentile Christianity in Conflict

Think with me for a few minutes about what it would have been like to be a Jew during Christ's time. Their history was extremely important to them. Centuries earlier God had called Abraham and promised to make of him a great nation, and they were that nation.

Suppose that early in our history God had said through Ellen White to Seventh-day Adventists, "I'm going to make you a great church." What would we think of ourselves today?

Later God delivered the Israelites—Abraham's descendants—from Egypt and gave them the Promised Land. Again and again He told them that they were His chosen people. They were very special, and He loved them above all other people in the whole world.

Suppose that through Ellen White God had said, "You are my special church. I chose you because I love you above all other churches in the world."

Then God gave the Israelites the great king David and told them that from David's descendants the Messiah would come to rule all nations.

Suppose God had said to Seventh-day Adventists, "I am going to raise up among you a great leader. Through his guidance the Seventh-day Adventist Church will become the greatest of all churches. It will rule all other churches in the world."

What would we think of ourselves if we had received such promises? Those of us who believed them would be tempted to think that we were somehow better than anyone else.

That is, in fact, what happened to the Jews after they returned from Babylonian captivity. At Christ's time their national identity, their religious prejudices, and their desire for ritual purity were so strong that they refused to associate socially with Gentiles.*

The Jews at Christ's time also had a keen sense that the Messiah was about to come and that the promise to Abraham that they would be the greatest nation in the world was about to be fulfilled. Their Messiah would be the universal ruler.

Jesus' disciples were infected with these ideas. They quarreled among themselves about which one of them would be the greatest in the coming kingdom—about who would be the prime minister, the chancellor of the exchequer, the secretary of state. They had all these offices divided up in their minds, and of course, each one was sure he would be prime minister.

Jesus' death crushed these fond hopes. They said, "We had hoped that he was the one who was going to redeem Israel" (Luke 24:21). When Jesus rose from the dead, their hopes revived. In Acts 1:6 we read that they said to Jesus, "Lord, are you at this time going to restore the kingdom to Israel?"

It's easy to miss the significance of that question. The disciples hoped, of course, that the Roman yoke would be broken and that Israel would be restored as an independent nation. But Old Testament prophecy did not just promise that Israel would be an independent nation at the end of time. God had promised that Israel would eventually become the head of all nations, and that all nations would come to Jerusalem to worship (see, for example, Isa. 60, especially verses 10-14). So when the disciples asked Jesus, "Will You at this time restore the kingdom to Israel?" they really meant, "Is this the time of the end, when Israel will become the head of all nations?"

And that's what Galatians is all about. You won't read anything about end-time events in Galatians, to be sure, nor will you read anything about Israel being the world's leading nation. But the assumption that this was Israel's destiny lay at the foundation of the whole debate. God's promises to the Jews, which convinced them that theirs was the only true religion, were so ingrained in the Jewish mind that even the apostles overcame this attitude only with great difficulty, and many Jewish Christians never did. It is impossible to fully understand Galatians apart from this backdrop.

In response to the disciples' question about whether He was about to establish His kingdom, Jesus said, "It is not for you to know the time or dates the Father has set by his own authority. But you will receive power when the Holy Spirit comes on you, and you will be my witnesses in Jerusalem, and all Judea and Samaria, and to the ends of the earth" (Acts 1:7, 8).

Notice that Jesus said the apostles were to preach the gospel in Jerusalem first, then in Judea and Samaria, and finally "to the ends of the earth." By "the ends of the earth" He meant that the gospel would be preached to Gentiles, and Gentiles would become Christians. However, the preaching was to commence in Jerusalem and Judea and move into Samaria before going to the Gentiles.

As we read through Acts, we discover that this is exactly what happened. The gospel was first preached in Jerusalem. The huge influx of believers on the day of Pentecost occurred in Jerusalem. Peter and John healed a lame man in Jerusalem. They gave their bold defense before the Sanhedrin in Jerusalem. The seven deacons were appointed in Jerusalem. The first six or seven chapters of Acts tell us about the earliest New Testament church in Jerusalem.

Acts makes only one slight reference about the spread of Christianity into Judea (see Acts 8:1). Apparently the stoning of Stephen precipitated a great persecution against the church. As a result, many Christians were scattered throughout Judea and Samaria. Wherever they went they spread the word about Jesus, which was, of course, the reason God allowed the persecution to happen. In Acts 8:5 we learn that Philip went down to a city in Samaria and proclaimed Christ. Apparently he was the first church leader to do that. As a result of his preaching, many demon-possessed people were set free, and paralytics and cripples were healed. The Bible says that "there was great joy in that city" (verse 8).

I think Luke had a reason for telling us about these miracles. As a Gentile author he wanted to be sure his readers understood that God Himself led these earliest Christians to preach the gospel to non-Jews.

When the apostles in Jerusalem heard that Samaria had accepted the Word of God, they sent Peter and John, the two highest officials in the Christian church in Jerusalem, on a fact-finding mission. The president and vice president of the General Conference went down to see what was happening in Samaria. This was obviously important! Luke wanted his readers to know that the evangelistic success in Samaria was not something that happened in a corner.

When Peter and John arrived they prayed for the Samaritans, that they might receive the Holy Spirit, and wonder of wonders—it happened. God blessed the Samaritans the same way He had blessed Jews who accepted Christ!

Luke also went out of his way to tell us that the Holy Spirit sent Philip into the wilderness on what must surely have seemed a very strange evangelistic project. Philip saw a chariot off in the distance, and the Spirit said,

"Go to that chariot and stay near it" (verse 29).

As Philip approached the chariot, he heard a Black man—an Ethiopian—reading a prophecy from Isaiah about the Messiah. Philip gave the man a Bible study and then baptized him. Again the Spirit had led in the conversion of a non-Jew.

I believe that Jesus had a reason for the geographical progression—Jerusalem, Judea, Samaria, the rest of the world—that He outlined in Acts 1:8 for the spread of the gospel. Jerusalem was the most convenient place to begin. The apostles were able to preach in their own culture, winning their own people. The gospel was preached exclusively to Jews during the first three or four years after Pentecost.

Even when it was time for the gospel to spread beyond Jewish borders, God did not launch His church straight into Gentile territory. Instead, He led His people gently to the next geographical group. Despite the deep Jewish antagonism toward Samaritans, the Samaritans were at least circumcised.

As the disciples spread out through Asia Minor, even then they began their missionary activities in the synagogues. If the Jews did not accept their gospel, the proselytes often did—just like the Ethiopian eunuch, who was probably a Jewish proselyte. Notice that there was one thing in common—Jews, Samaritans, and proselytes were all circumcised. The Jewish Christians in Jerusalem could say, "The Samaritans are circumcised, and the proselytes and this eunuch were circumcised, so that's OK."

But God didn't stop there. Peter was in Joppa one day, atop the roof on the home of a friend, when the Spirit told him to go downstairs and meet some guests. The men Peter met at the gate took him to Caesarea, to the home of a Roman centurion. This man was a Gentile, and a good Jew did not socialize with Gentiles. Peter must have felt nervous as he entered the home. But when he got inside he found the house full of Gentiles—and the Spirit had led him into this situation!

Peter apparently had some associates with him, and they no doubt felt uneasy too. But an amazing thing happened. While Peter was speaking to the people, the Holy Spirit came upon everyone, and the Gentiles spoke in tongues. The Jewish believers who had come with Peter were astonished that the gift of the Holy Spirit had been poured out even on Gentiles. Then Peter said, "Can anyone keep these people from being baptized with water? They have received the Holy Spirit just as we have" (Acts 10:47). And he ordered that they be baptized in the name of Jesus.

As soon as Peter got back to Jerusalem the word got around quickly that he of all people had been in the home of a Gentile and that he had even baptized Gentiles. This news caused such an uproar that the leadership of the church called a business meeting. "Peter," they said, "you've got to explain yourself. Why did you go into the house of uncircumcised men and eat with them, and why, of *all* things, did you baptize them?"

Do you see the tension building? It was OK to baptize Samaritans and a converted Ethiopian. They were circumcised. But Cornelius was an uncircumcised Gentile, and the right-wing Jewish Christians simply could not tolerate his baptism.

Peter explained everything that had happened. "As I began to speak," he said, "the Holy Spirit came on them as he had come on us at the beginning. Then I remembered what the Lord had said: 'John baptized with water, but you will be baptized with the Holy Spirit.' So if God gave them the same gift as he gave us, who believed in the Lord Jesus Christ, who was I to think that I could oppose God?" (Acts 11:15-17).

When the participants at the business meeting heard Peter's defense they had no further objection. To the contrary, they praised God, saying, "So then, God has granted even the Gentiles repentance unto life" (verse 18). To them this was utterly amazing, but true.

Luke was making an important point here. He wanted his readers to understand that at every step the leadership of the early Christian church accepted the progress of the gospel to the Gentiles. Yet even here God led His people gently. Cornelius was a Gentile, but he was also a Jewish sympathizer (see Acts 10:1, 2), which made his reception of the Holy Spirit a little more tolerable. This was different from going into raw Gentile territory and bringing pagans directly into Christianity.

However, God soon showed that He wanted His church to take that step, too. Those who had been scattered by the persecution in connection with Stephen's death traveled as far as Phoenicia, Cyprus, and Antioch, spreading the message about Jesus—but only to Jews (see Acts 11:19). They still didn't understand that they had a mission to the Gentile world. A few, however, went to Antioch and began speaking to Greeks also. The Bible says that "the Lord's hand was with them, and a great number of people believed and turned to the Lord" (verse 21).

Again the news reached the ears of the church in Jerusalem, and they sent Barnabas to Antioch. When Barnabas "arrived and saw the evidence of the grace of God, he was glad and encouraged them all [the Gentile converts] to remain true to the Lord with all their hearts" (Acts 11:22, 23). So many people accepted Christ that Barnabas needed help. And since he was in Gentile territory, he went after the best help he could get for reaching Gentiles. Saul had been preaching in Tarsus for several years, and Barnabas invited him to come to Antioch. Saul accepted the invitation, and he and Barnabas labored successfully for a whole year.

Now the church was ready for the big push into Gentile territory. Not everyone was ready, as we shall soon see, but enough of the church's top leadership and of the membership at large were spiritually and emotionally prepared that the opposition could not block the effort.

In Acts 13:1, 2 we read that God led certain prophets and teachers in Antioch to set aside Barnabas and Saul with fasting and prayer and the laying on of hands, after which they sent them on a long preaching tour in Gentile territory. Notice that before Luke told the story about Paul's first missionary journey he assured his readers that Paul went under the direction of the Holy Spirit.

I won't go into all the details of Paul's first missionary journey. Suffice it to say that it was imminently successful. Many people were baptized, and many new churches were established. It may have been on this journey that Paul established the church in Galatia, though Luke did not mention it.

At the conclusion of their evangelistic tour, Paul and his companions returned to Antioch, where they gathered the church together and reported all that God had done among the Gentiles through them. Luke did not give the slightest hint that the Christians in Antioch were anything but overjoyed at the success of Paul's missionary journey. And for good reason: the church at Antioch was composed largely of Gentile believers, not Jews. They would naturally have been thrilled with Paul's report.

However, it was not long before word of Paul's missionary tour reached Jerusalem, and the Jewish party was not nearly so thrilled. A certain group of them felt particularly disturbed, and they sent a delegation to Antioch. They didn't directly confront Paul and the other leaders, though. They just infiltrated the church. The Bible says that "some men came down from Judea to Antioch and were teaching the brothers: 'Unless you are circumcised according to the custom taught by Moses, you cannot be saved'" (Acts 15:1).

The contention between Paul and this Jewish party became so sharp that the church appointed Paul and Barnabas and several other leaders to go to Jerusalem and consult with the apostles and elders about this question.

Luke says that "as they traveled through Phoenicia and Samaria, they told how the Gentiles had been converted. This news made all the brothers very glad" (verse 3). Luke wanted his readers to know that the Jewish party was a small faction; the majority of Christians felt inspired by Paul's report. He also made a point of the fact that when the delegation from Antioch arrived in Jerusalem "they were welcomed by the church and the apostles and elders, to whom they reported everything God had done through them" (verse 4).

The apostles convened a meeting to hear both sides of the conflict centered in Antioch. This meeting has come to be known as the Jerusalem Council. The Bible says that the Pharisees stood up and said, "The Gentiles must be circumcised and required to obey the law of Moses" (verse 5). But Peter replied that through him God had brought the Holy Spirit into the hearts of Gentile believers. (He was referring, of course, to his experience with Cornelius.) Why, then, Peter reasoned, should the church expect Gentiles to become Jews in order to become Christians?

When a vote was taken, the leadership in Jerusalem sanctioned what Paul had been doing. Several representatives from Jerusalem were appointed to return to Antioch with Paul and his companions to settle the problem there. When the Antioch Christians received the report of the Jerusalem Council they were pleased.

This is the background we need in order to understand Galatians. When we get into Paul's letter to the Galatians, you will discover that he Jewish party that caused trouble in Antioch did not sit idly by just because the Jerusalem Council authorized Paul's preaching to Gentiles. They dogged Paul's steps throughout the Roman Empire, and they especially seem to have had a strong influence on the minds of the Galatian Christians.

---

*Business dealings were, of course, necessary and thus allowed. Interaction for social purposes, such as eating together, was the taboo.

CHAPTER 2

Called to Be an Apostle
Galatians 1

The first century was the most ideal period in Christian history. With the apostles around to guide, and with the Holy Spirit filling every Christian's heart with Pentecostal power, God's people lived in perfect peace and harmony.

Right?

Wrong!

Serious divisions split some congregations right down the middle. A quarrel over equal rights broke out very early in the church at Jerusalem, and the church in Corinth kept up a running battle over who was the best preacher (see Acts 6:1; 1 Cor. 1:10-17). Worst of all, as we found out in the previous chapter, the conflict over the conversion of Gentiles to Christ divided the entire Christian community.

The Galatian congregation in particular seems to have been plagued with this conflict. Since Paul raised up this congregation (see Gal. 4:13), he naturally felt anxious about its well-being. His Epistle to the Galatians was his defense of the gospel that he had preached there and his appeal for them to remain faithful to it.

It is important to understand that Galatians gives us only Paul's view of the conflict in Galatia. We have no direct information about the arguments of his opponents. We could wish we had an epistle to the Galatians from the leader of the Jewish party. Since we have only Paul's side of the debate, we have to depend on him to provide us with the arguments made by the Jewish party. Unfortunately for us, for the most part Paul assumed that his readers were familiar with those arguments, and he responded to them without stating them. About the best we can do is to infer the arguments made by the Jewish party from a careful reading of Paul's response. Keeping this in mind will help us deal with some of the problems we find in his letter.

We are, in fact, confronted with this difficulty in the first verse of chapter 1. Apparently the Jewish party claimed that Paul received his commission to preach to the Gentiles from some human source. But Paul insisted that he was "an apostle—sent not from men nor by man, but by Jesus Christ and God the Father."

Paul often introduced himself in his letters as an apostle, and he usually stressed that he was an apostle "by the will of God." Notice, for instance, the following:

- Romans 1:1—"Paul, a servant of Christ Jesus, called to be an apostle and set apart for the gospel of God."
- 1 Corinthians 1:1—"Paul, called to be an apostle of Christ Jesus by the will of God."
- Ephesians 1:1—"Paul, an apostle of Christ Jesus by the will of God."

It seems likely that another of the Jewish party's major arguments against Paul was his lack of credentials as an apostle. It is important to understand that in a very real sense the Jewish party had a valid point, at least by the definition of "apostle" that was adopted in the earliest days of the church's existence. After Jesus ascended to heaven, but before Pentecost, Peter proposed that the group replace Judas with "one of the men who have been with us the whole time the Lord Jesus went in and out among us, beginning from John's baptism to the time when Jesus was taken up from us. For one of these must become a witness with us of his resurrection" (Acts 1:21).

Notice two things about the qualifications of an apostle in Peter's statement: He must have walked and talked with Jesus for three and a half years, and he must have witnessed Him in His resurrected body. Paul failed on both counts. Paul could not say with Peter, "We were eyewitnesses of his majesty" (2 Peter 1:16), nor could he say with John, "That which . . . we have heard, which we have seen with our eyes, which we have looked at and our hands have touched" (1 John 1:1).

Nowhere in the New Testament do we find an accusation by a member of the Jewish party saying that Paul was unqualified to be an apostle because he had not spent time personally with Jesus while He was on earth. But Paul's repeated defense of his apostolic ministry should lead us to suspect that that was indeed one of their major arguments.

Paul responded by emphasizing again and again that he received his call directly from Jesus Christ—meaning, of course, his experience on the road to Damascus. Because of this, he claimed a right to be called an apostle every bit as much as any of the twelve.

Paul's rejection by the Jewish party carries an important lesson for us today. Every now and then during the years I spent as a pastor I ran into someone who would say, "God has called me to do such and such," and the person would get upset if the church did not recognize that call and immediately give him or her a job. This is often a problem with young people who feel called to the ministry. Church leaders sometimes question the qualifications of certain persons, which, of course, makes these young people feel discouraged. This is understandable. I'm sure I'd be discouraged too.

But Paul was never deterred by the fact that some people questioned his call to the ministry. This will become increasingly clear as we get into Galatians.

In Galatians 1:3-5 Paul said: "Grace and peace to you from God our Father and the Lord Jesus Christ, who gave himself for our sins to rescue us from the present evil age, according to the will of our God and Father, to whom be glory for ever and ever. Amen."

The words "grace and peace to you" are a greeting, something like when we say "Hello" or "How are you?" Paul often used this greeting in his letters.

In our culture "How are you?" is just a formality. What we really mean is "I see you and I'm letting you know that, because if I failed to acknowledge your presence you'd think I was rude."

And the person who says "I'm just fine, thank you" really means "I feel terrible right now, and I'd just as soon not waste the energy to greet you. But then you'd think *I* was rude, so I'll tell you I'm fine just to keep myself in your good graces."

I have exaggerated, of course, but you get the point. Often the words we say in a greeting are a formality. We don't really mean them. Usually we say them automatically, without even thinking.

The question we have to ask as we read Paul's greeting in nearly every one of his letters is Are his words a mere formality, or does he really mean them? "Grace" was a common Greek greeting (*charein*), sort of like our hello, and the common Hebrew greeting was "peace" (*shalom*). Peter and John also used this combined greeting (see 1 Peter 1:2; 2 Peter 1:2; 2 John 3; Rev. 1:4). Apparently it was a common New Testament salutation, reflecting the dual Jewish and Gentile makeup of the church.

No doubt these words *were* often spoken as a greeting in which the words did not necessarily reflect the speaker's real feelings at the moment.

However, I think we can safely say that Paul really wanted the Christians who read his letters to experience God's grace. He wanted them to understand the reality of the peace that could be theirs through Jesus Christ. He wanted them to understand that Jesus really did give Himself for their sins to rescue them from the evil in the world.

Please notice something interesting, though. Compare Paul's introductory comments in Galatians with the introductory comments in some of his other letters. I will repeat Galatians 1:3-5: "Grace and peace to you from God our Father and the Lord Jesus Christ, who gave himself for our sins to rescue us from the present evil age, according to the will of our God and Father, to whom be glory for ever and ever. Amen."

Compare these remarks with Paul's introductions in the following letters:

- Romans 1:8—"First, I thank my God through Jesus Christ for all of you, because your faith is being reported all over the world."
- 1 Corinthians 1:4—"I always thank God for you because of his grace given you in Christ Jesus."
- Philippians 1:3—"I thank my God every time I remember you."

Notice that Paul did not say "I thank my God for you Galatians." Why? Because he knew that these people were on their way to apostasy. He didn't tell us whether he thought the Galatians were undeserving of his prayers of thanksgiving or whether he was in such a hurry to get on with his letter that he forgot to tell them he thanked God for them. Either way, I think we can safely assume that Paul did pray for his Galatian friends, the way a parent prays for a wayward son or daughter. He probably prayed *more* for the Galatian Christians at this time than for any other church members.

In Galatians 1:6 Paul launched directly into his subject. "I am astonished that you are so quickly deserting the one who called you by the grace of Christ and are turning to a different gospel." Right from the start Paul said, "There's a problem here." He didn't try to be diplomatic. He just said it.

When he said, "You are so quickly deserting the one who called you by the grace of Christ," was he talking about himself or about God? Of course, God calls every Christian. But it seems to me that Paul was talking about himself, because he said, "You are so quickly deserting *the one who called you* by the *grace of Christ*." God has never needed the grace of Christ to call people. Paul did.

Then Paul said to the Christians in Galatia: "You are . . . turning to a different gospel—which is really no gospel at all. Evidently some people are throwing you into confusion and are trying to pervert the gospel of Christ. But even if we or an angel from heaven should preach a gospel other than the one we preached to you, let him be eternally condemned! As we have already said, so now I say again: If anybody is preaching to you a gospel other than what you accepted [meaning what you accepted from me], let him be eternally condemned!" (verses 6-9).

That is *very* strong language. Even though he didn't name them, Paul was talking about the Jewish party. These people had infiltrated the Galatian church and had gotten many of the Gentile believers to think that they had to become Jews in order to be good Christians. They insisted that Gentiles had to be circumcised and keep all the ceremonial laws and Jewish feast days.[1] Paul called this "a different gospel—which is really no gospel at all." He said that "some people [the Jewish party] are throwing you into confusion."

It is crucial to understand that the people from the Jewish party who came into Galatia were sincere in their convictions. They believed with all their hearts that their message was essential to true spiritual life and eternal salvation. Yet according to Paul they were absolutely wrong—so wrong that Paul said anyone who preached their message was eternally condemned! And to be sure his readers got the point, he said it twice.

Think of it. These people were utterly sincere, convinced that they were right. They claimed to be acting from all the best motives, with nothing but the best interests of the Gentile Christians in Galatia at heart. They wanted these people to have the healthiest, happiest religious experience. Yet Paul said, "You are utterly wrong." And because we accept Paul as an apostle of Christ, we believe he was right.

Let's take a moment to apply this to our situation. Sometimes people come into the Adventist Church and say, "You have to do this, or you have to do that, or you have to believe this or that. If you don't believe and do things my way, you are wrong and are endangering your eternal salvation." Often these people—these parties in our church—seem to be utterly sincere. They claim to have the best interests of the church at heart. Yet in an unfortunate number of cases these people are absolutely wrong.

Verses 11, 12 get us to the heart of the matter—the gospel. "I want you to know, brothers," Paul said, "that the gospel I preached is not something that man made up. I did not receive it from any man, nor was I taught it;

rather, I received it by revelation from Jesus Christ."

Why did Paul say "I did not receive it from any man, nor was I taught it"?

As part of their strategy to discount Paul's claim that God had called him to the apostolic ministry, the Jewish party apparently said he learned his gospel from persons whom they considered to be renegade Christians. And as we will see in Galatians 2, the renegade Christians they had in mind were none other than the two top leaders of the church in Jerusalem—Peter and James.[2]

Paul replied by claiming that he had received his gospel directly from God through a divine revelation.

Had Paul been given a vision? Had God spoken to him? Had an angel taught him? Any of these could be called a revelation. Paul did not tell us exactly how his revelation came. However, the revelation he mentioned in verse 12 is one of two revelations from God that he spoke about in Galatians. He mentioned the other one in chapter 2.

The Jewish party disputed Paul's claim that he had received his gospel by a revelation from God. How could Paul prove that he had? He couldn't, of course—not with any objective evidence. The Jewish party, the Gentiles, and you and I can only accept Paul's claim by faith.

Can Adventists prove that God spoke through Ellen White? Can the Mormons prove that God spoke through Joseph Smith? No. We can only accept these prophets by faith, and Adventists reject the Mormon claim that Joseph Smith was a prophet because we do not have their faith.

In verses 13, 14 Paul began defending his apostleship with a bit of personal history. He said: "For you have heard of my previous way of life in Judaism, how intensely I persecuted the church of God and tried to destroy it. I was advancing in Judaism beyond many Jews of my own age and was extremely zealous for the traditions of my fathers."

Why do you suppose Paul spoke about his former persecution of Christians? Keep in mind that he was defending his claim to be an apostle called by God. I think we can paraphrase his logic something like this: "The Jewish party thinks I received my gospel from men, but that doesn't make sense. I persecuted the church. I was ahead of most of my countrymen in defending Judaism. Any human being who was *that* steeped in his religion would not allow himself to be changed by mere human influence. My change *had* to come from God. And that revelation I just mentioned is where God talked to me about the new doctrines He wanted me to teach."

Next Paul turned to his Damascus road experience and the days and years that followed to substantiate that his gospel did not originate with the church's leadership in Jerusalem: "But when God, who set me apart from birth and called me by his grace, was pleased to reveal his Son in me so that I might preach him among the Gentiles, I did not consult any man, nor did I go up to Jerusalem to see those who were apostles before I was, but I went immediately into Arabia and later returned to Damascus" (verses 15-17).

Paul said, in effect, "How can you pharisaical Jews say that my gospel came from men when I didn't consult with anyone after my conversion? I didn't even go to Jerusalem to see the apostles. I went directly into Arabia, and then I returned to Damascus."

In verse 18 Paul said that after three years he did go to Jerusalem, but this could hardly be construed as evidence that he received his gospel from the church's leadership, because the only leaders he spoke with were Peter and James, and he stayed with them just 15 days. His point seems to be, "What do you mean I got my doctrine from men when I spent only two weeks in Jerusalem and consulted with only two of the apostles?"

Apparently Paul had told this story before, and the Jewish party had disputed his account of the facts, because he responded in verse 20: "I assure you before God that what I am writing you is no lie."

Paul really got worked up!

But he still wasn't through sharing with the Galatians his personal history. From his visit in Jerusalem with Peter and James, he went to Syria and Cilicia. Where are Syria and Cilicia? You will recall that the eastern shore of the Mediterranean Sea runs from Egypt pretty much straight north along the coast of Palestine to Turkey. If you keep going straight inland into Turkey, you'll soon reach the region of ancient Syria and Cilicia, which is also where Paul's childhood home of Tarsus was located. He spent many years preaching the gospel in that region (see Gal. 2:1).

Paul concluded chapter 1 by saying, "I was personally unknown to the churches of Judea that are in Christ. They only heard the report: 'The man who formerly persecuted us is preaching the faith he once tried to destroy'" (verses 22, 23).

And then he said something interesting: "And they praised God because of me" (verse 24). Syria and Cilicia were Gentile territory, and, faithful to his call, Paul would have worked largely among Gentiles. By showing how the Judean Christians praised God for his ministry to the

Gentiles, Paul was isolating the Jewish party as a small minority even among the Jewish churches in Judea.

Earlier in this chapter I raised the question "What should Christians do who feel called to do a certain work for God but the church fails to recognize that call by giving them jobs?"

We are now in a good position to answer that question. What did Paul do when he received God's call to preach to the Gentiles? One of the most obvious conclusions is that the leadership in Jerusalem did not snap to attention and say "How wonderful, Paul, that God has given you this ministry to the Gentiles! We'll put you on the payroll right away, complete with a travel budget and per diem. Your territory will be the Southern European Division." To the contrary, God sent Paul into the Arabian desert!

So if you feel called by God and if the church does not recognize that call, if you feel that instead you have been pushed off into the "wilderness" somewhere, just remember Paul. God sent him into a blazing hot desert! After your desert experience—or even while it's going on—follow Paul's example. He didn't need a call from the church. When God called him, he rolled up his sleeves and went to work as a layman.

After Paul had proved himself for many years, the church ordained him and sent him off on his first missionary journey. Yet even after he had received this formal recognition, he encountered serious opposition from the Jewish party. So don't be surprised if, after the church finally recognizes your call, you still encounter opposition from some people. That's exactly what happened to Paul, yet he never lost his personal sense of assurance that he was doing God's work. Because of that assurance, he was able to meet the opposition boldly.

Here's another practical question that arises out of our study of the Jewish party's attack on Paul: In our zeal for the purity of the church, are you and I ever guilty of making unchristian attacks on those with whom we disagree? This is a very relevant question in the Adventist Church today. I've heard some of the most vicious attacks on the church from people who claim to be Christians, who claim to have in mind the best interests of the church. In fact, I've personally experienced some of these attacks.

Like the Jewish party, certain people in the Seventh-day Adventist Church are extremely zealous for their particular form of theology—so zealous that sometimes they advance their views in unethical ways. They become angry with and condemn anyone who disagrees with them. I have to question anybody's theology, regardless of how correct it may be, who talks like that. I have to question the theology and especially the motives of people who get angry at other Christians simply because these other Christians don't agree with them on a particular point of doctrine.

Apparently a large number of Galatian Christians accepted the message of the Jewish party when they came to town. They failed to recognize the false gospel. The question is Could they have recognized the error? And the answer is yes. That's why God gave spiritual gifts to the church: "It was he who gave some to be apostles, some to be prophets, some to be evangelists, and some to be pastors and teachers. . . . Then we will no longer be infants, tossed back and forth by the waves, and blown here and there by every wind of teaching and by the cunning and craftiness of men in their deceitful scheming" (Eph. 4:11-14).

The Galatian Christians were blown back and forth by the wind of teaching of the Jewish party. Fortunately Paul had the spiritual gifts of apostleship, knowledge, teaching, and prophecy. He used all these gifts to settle the problem in Galatia. When the church in Galatia received Paul's letter, did they settle down? I hope so. I hope that this letter brought unity and stability. I hope that from then on they were less susceptible to "every wind of teaching." That's one of the major purposes of spiritual gifts, and I believe that Paul's spiritual gifts did make that possible in the Galatian church.

I also hope that within a few years of receiving Paul's letter the Galatian Christians had built their own corps of men and women with spiritual gifts, who could protect them from falling into the next doctrinal trap.

Most of all, I hope that both you and your church are spiritually strong and that you will use your spiritual gifts to protect your church from being "blown here and there by every wind of teaching."

---

[1] I will point out repeatedly in this book that the ultimate issue with the Jewish party was the law and their religion as a whole, yet I will also state that the Jewish party seemed obsessed with just the ceremonial aspects of that law. The answer to this apparent inconsistency lies, I believe, in understanding that the ceremonial aspects of that law were the Jewish party's measure of one's loyalty to the system as a whole. Similarly, the issue with Adventist legalists is Adventism as a whole, with standards as a measure of one's loyalty to all that Adventism stands for.

[2] I do not mean that Peter and James were renegade Christians. They both gave their full support to Paul at the Jerusalem Council. But it was precisely their support of Paul that caused the Jewish party to view them as "renegade." They had abandoned "the true faith."

Contending for the Faith
Galatians 2:1-14

During the time I was writing the first chapters of this book, a friend sent me a taped sermon by someone associated with an Adventist independent ministry. The speaker began his remarks with a scathing rebuke of people who teach a certain doctrine that he claimed was false. "If we would just study the Bible," he avowed, "we would all realize that the doctrine we are being taught is contrary to the Word of God."

I could not help thinking of a videotape I had seen some months earlier, put out by another Adventist independent ministry, defending the very teaching that the tape I was now listening to condemned. I was particularly impressed by the fact that both speakers, before they began their sermons, prayed earnestly that God would "reveal His truth today." And I wondered which prayer the Lord heard.

Since I am neither in favor of nor opposed to the particular doctrine in question (I don't think it can be proved either way, and it definitely is not a matter of salvation), I listened to both sides rather dispassionately. Probably my major feeling was amusement that people on each side of a controversial question should become so worked up, each absolutely certain that because he had the truth, God surely must be on his side.

This experience underscores, I think, what was happening in the church at Galatia. We, of course, believe that there was a right and a wrong side to the issue in that congregation. But the point is that the Jewish party felt absolutely certain they were right, and apparently they opposed Paul with a passion born of utter conviction to the day of his death.

Our first reaction is to deplore such situations. It's particularly easy for us to deplore the Jewish-Gentile conflict in the early church, since we know that one side was unquestionably in the right and the other wrong. "Why was the Jewish party so blind?" we ask, as though we surely would not have been so blind had we been in their shoes. And we shake our heads that such a situation should have arisen in the first place.

However, I believe that disagreement among sincere Christians over doctrinal questions is a normal part of church life, even among those who have the best interests of God's work at heart. Differences of opinion are to be expected, and even welcomed. People who care about their church question those who differ with them on important doctrinal matters. This is one sign of a healthy church. God leads His church through these disagreements to a better understanding of truth.

Even when one party to a disagreement is clearly in the wrong, his or her insistence on that particular point of view pushes those whose view may be closer to the truth to study their position more carefully. Without the Jewish party's insistence on their views, which nearly all Christians today recognize were false, we would not have Paul's letter to the Galatians, and Christians for nearly 2,000 years would have been the losers.

However, I am sure few of us today want to benefit future generations of Christians by taking the wrong side of an argument! Everyone wants to be on the right side. The question is How can we be sure which side of a deeply controversial issue is the proper one, when apparently good people on each side present such persuasive arguments?

The Galatian controversy provides us with an excellent biblical model for resolving doctrinal conflicts today and coming out on the correct side. In the New Testament church the Holy Spirit used three things to resolve these controversies: hard study, earnest deliberation by church leaders, and church authority. God is just as willing to use these processes to help Seventh-day Adventists settle doctrinal controversies now as He was 2,000 years ago. We *must* have confidence that God will lead us to understand the truth through these debates in which we sometimes become so emotionally embroiled.

Galatians 2 introduces us to God's way of helping His church settle doctrinal controversy. However, before we get into chapter 2, let's take a moment to review chapter 1. The Jewish party claimed that Paul got his gospel from men, but Paul said that God gave it to him—by revelation. He pointed out that it would have been impossible for him to have gotten his gospel from a human source, since he spent almost no time with church leaders and other Christians during the years immediately following his Damascus road experience. He concluded chapter 1 by pointing out that three years after his conversion he went to Syria and Cilicia in what would today be southeastern Turkey. And as all his readers would have known, there were no Christians in that region at the time except for those Paul himself converted after he got there.

Paul began chapter 2 by saying, "Fourteen years later I went up again to Jerusalem, this time with Barnabas. I took Titus along also" (verse 1). In Galatians 1 Paul's argument was "I went all this time without consulting the leadership in Jerusalem." In Galatians 2 he switched to "Look what they said when I did finally see them."

Did Paul actually spend all 14 years preaching the gospel in Syria and Cilicia? Probably not. In Acts 11:19-26 we learn that after the Christian message took root in Antioch, Barnabas visited the city. He found such an interest among the Greek population that he was unable to handle all the evangelistic work himself. He brought in Paul to help him, and they worked together for a year. So at the very most Paul would have spent 13 years in Syria and Cilicia before making the trip to Jerusalem that he mentioned in Galatians 2.

But when *did* Paul take that trip to Jerusalem? There are two possibilities.

Acts 11:27-30 tells us that during the year Paul and Barnabas worked together in Antioch, the church sent the two of them to Jerusalem with a famine relief offering. This would have been a short time *before* his first missionary journey. Some scholars believe that this is the Jerusalem visit Paul mentioned in Galatians 2. However, there is another possibility. Acts 15 tells about Paul's defense of his gospel before the church leadership in Jerusalem shortly *after* his first missionary journey, and other scholars believe that this is the Jerusalem visit Paul described in Galatians 2. My personal conclusion is that Paul's Galatians 2 visit corresponded to the Jerusalem visit that Luke mentioned in Acts 11, *before* his first missionary journey, but that Paul probably wrote his letter to the Galatians *after* he had attended the Jerusalem Council of Acts 15. Fortunately, we do not have to settle this question in order to reach an adequate interpretation of Galatians.*

In Galatians 2:2 Paul made a significant statement. He said that he went to Jerusalem after 14 years in Syria and Cilicia "in response to a revelation," and he emphasized that the purpose of this visit was to "set before them [the leadership in Jerusalem] the gospel that I preach among the Gentiles" (verse 2). I believe this gives us an important principle for settling doctrinal differences. Paul's whole point in Galatians 1 was that he had received his gospel directly from God through a revelation, and not from any human source. Yet in Galatians 2 God gave him another revelation in which He said, in essence, "Now I want you to go and get the church's leadership to confirm this gospel I have revealed to you."

God does not work apart from His church. He does not work apart from His appointed leaders. This does not mean that church leadership is perfect, nor does it mean that it is impossible for a church and its leadership to apostatize to the point that God can no longer use them. But this level of apostasy takes many centuries. It had not happened in the short history of the New Testament church when Paul first went to Jerusalem. Nor, I believe, has it happened to the Seventh-day Adventist Church today.

If God directed Paul (to whom He gave a personal revelation of the gospel) to have that gospel confirmed by the church's leadership, then I believe He wants us today to do the same. This does not mean that we must all teach the same doctrine down to the last detail, nor does it mean that the General Conference president and his corps of officers must be the final arbiters of all doctrinal differences. The General Conference officers I've known don't want that responsibility. They recognize that there is room for disagreement on the nonessentials. But on the central teachings of the church, the General Conference in session must have the last word, and the church around the world must unite around that body of teaching. If God were to instruct one of us through a revelation to have our teaching confirmed by the church the way He did Paul in Galatians 2, He might well ask us to present our views to the church's leadership first, particularly those who have been charged with the responsibility of responding to variations in doctrinal teaching.

Some people among us don't like this idea. They are convinced that their teaching is correct, and they don't want to submit their views to the church's leadership. But I think it is extremely significant that after God revealed the gospel to Paul, He then said, "Now go get it approved by the church." This, I believe, is a model we need to follow today.

Next Paul brought up the case of Titus, who was a Gentile and therefore uncircumcised: "Yet not even Titus, who was with me, was compelled to be circumcised, even though he was a Greek" (verse 3).

Paul may have brought Titus along with him to Jerusalem as a test case, to see what the leadership of the church in Jerusalem would do. He probably felt quite certain that the Jewish party would object to Titus' presence among Jewish Christians, and if so, his suspicions were rewarded. However, if we read between the lines of Paul's story, it appears that the Jewish party decided to confirm that Titus really was uncircumcised before coming forth with their objections. After all, they didn't want to challenge Paul for bringing in an uncircumcised Gentile only to have Paul say, "You're wrong; Titus has been circumcised." So to protect themselves, they decided to do a little investigating first.

The easiest way to find out about Titus' status would have been to ask, of course, but the Jewish party resorted to sleuthing instead. Paul said: "This matter arose because some false brothers had infiltrated our ranks to spy on the freedom we have in Christ Jesus and make us slaves" (verse 4).

This act of spying on the part of the Jewish party is an indication of their motives. Why didn't they ask Paul and Titus point blank whether Titus had been circumcised? I have no doubt that Paul would have been glad to report the facts. He might even have recommended that Titus submit to a physical examination. The fact that they resorted to spying suggests that they were not as interested in determining God's will as they were in advancing their own cause. Yet the major issue they made of this case clarified, as nothing else could have, that the top leadership of the Christian church accepted the principle that Gentile Christians need not submit to circumcision, for Paul reported that "not even Titus, who was with me, was compelled to be circumcised, even though he was a Greek." By forcing the issue with their unethical spying, the Jewish party made their loss and our gain greater than if they had kept silent.

Let's take a moment to review Paul's argument so far in Galatians. His major point in chapter 1 was that the Jewish party's claim that he had received his gospel from some human source was a historical impossibility. To the contrary, he got it by direct revelation from God. In chapter 2 he acknowledged finally going to Jerusalem—but not to receive his gospel *from* the church's leadership; rather, he went to present to them the gospel he'd been preaching all along. He even took a test case along with him so that the decision the leaders made would be based on action, not just belief. And what was the result? "Those men added nothing to my message. On the contrary, they saw that I had been entrusted with the task of preaching the gospel to the Gentiles, just as Peter had been to the Jews. . . . [They] gave me and Barnabas the right hand of fellowship when they recognized the grace given to me. They agreed that we should go to the Gentiles, and they to the Jews" (verses 6-9).

I think it is important to notice that the early church's conflict over circumcision was not just a theological argument. It was a question of practice. The issue was not just What shall we all believe? but also What will we all do? We can debate profound theological issues until the Lord comes and remain fairly united. For instance, there is considerable discussion in the Adventist Church today over whether God will punish the wicked in the lake of fire or whether their death will simply be a natural result of their own sinfulness. This debate has nothing to do with anyone's behavior. It doesn't tell us what to eat or drink, when to go to bed, or when to go to work. As long as these theological discussions do not affect our behavior, we can disagree and walk away and forget about it. Nobody wins or loses as long as all we have to do is talk.

But when each side feels strongly that its way of *doing* something is the only right way and those on the other side are wrong, we can't disagree and forget about it. We may postpone taking action in an effort to negotiate a united front, but if a negotiated settlement is not forthcoming, sooner or later one side will almost certainly say, "We're going to act on our convictions." The side that acts first forces the issue to a resolution. If a uniform course of action is not forthcoming at that point, a church split may result.

Several years ago the Seventh-day Adventist Church faced an issue like that. The ordination of women to gospel ministry is not merely a theological debate. It involves action—whether or not to lay hands on female ministers. All along, the bottom line in this discussion was identical to the early Christian debate over circumcision: What will the body *do?*

I am glad that our church settled this question according to the New Testament model—a model that was given to Paul by a revelation from God Himself (verse 2). When Paul became embroiled in a heated disagreement with the Jewish party over the validity of his gospel, God said, "Let the church decide."

In the early church the decision was made by the leadership in Jerusalem—the equivalent, perhaps, of the officers of our General Conference. However, our church today settles deeply significant matters of belief and practice through an even wider representation. The question of the ordination of women was brought to the quinquennial session of the world body that met in Indianapolis in July 1990. You are no doubt aware that the vote, by a wide margin, was against ordination of women. Those who supported ordination of women were deeply disappointed, but by and large I believe they accepted the decision in a Christian spirit. I am thankful I belong to a church that can settle a deeply divisive issue according to the biblical model and remain united and committed to its ultimate task. I believe the Holy Spirit led in that decision, just as He led in the decision about circumcision nearly 2,000 years ago.

Unfortunately, the Jewish party did not accept the church's decision so graciously. To the contrary, they kept agitating their views. They kept unsettling churches. Paul told about a brief confrontation he had with them some time later in Antioch.

Peter had been one of the leaders in Jerusalem who accepted Paul's ministry to Gentiles, including the proviso that Gentiles need not be circumcised (see verse 9). Also, at the Jerusalem Council, Peter had made a strong speech in support of Paul's gospel (see Acts 15:6-11).

Later Peter visited the church at Antioch, and while he was there, some representatives of the Jewish party from Jerusalem showed up. Perhaps it was a potluck meal after the Sabbath services. Paul didn't inform us of the occasion. Whenever it was, though, the Jewish party insisted on eating at a table to themselves, away from the Gentile believers, and they invited Peter to join them. Paul was horrified when Peter accepted their invitation.

Under normal circumstances there would be nothing wrong with accepting the invitation of a small group of people to eat lunch together at a church potluck. But the Jewish party had set up a deliberate test case, just as Paul did when he took Titus with him to Jerusalem, and Peter fell into their trap. Unfortunately, other Jewish Christians followed Peter's example and separated themselves from the Gentiles. Even Barnabas, Paul's personal associate, compromised his principles.

Paul's response was immediate and decisive:

> When Peter came to Antioch, I opposed him to his face, because he was clearly in the wrong. Before certain men came from James, he used to eat with the Gentiles. But when they arrived, he began to draw back and separate himself from the Gentiles because he was afraid of those who belonged to the circumcision group. The other Jews joined him in his hypocrisy, so that by their hypocrisy even Barnabas was led astray.
>
> When I saw that they were not acting in line with the truth of the gospel, I said to Peter in front of them all, "You are a Jew,

yet you live like a Gentile and not like a Jew. How is it, then,
that you force Gentiles to follow Jewish customs?" (verses 11-14).

Our usual tendency when we are confronted with a behavior problem
in the church is to be diplomatic, to try to keep the controversy from
breaking out into the open. Sometimes that is an appropriate response.
But in this particular context, think of what Peter's actions said to all the
Gentiles who were at that meal. One day Peter ate with them and fellow-
shipped with them and was happy to call himself one of them. I'm sure
they all had a good time together. But the next day, when the Jewish party
arrived, Peter went off to eat with them and refused to associate with the
Gentiles. How do you think that made the Gentiles feel? Rejected, to say
the least.

It would have been bad enough had the issue been just a matter of the
feelings of Gentile Christians, but there was much more at stake than that.
Paul recognized that the real issue underlying Peter's behavior was the
church's support of the gospel that he (Paul) preached. Did Peter and the
church really mean it when they affirmed Paul's ministry to the Gentiles?
That was the real issue, and that's why Paul confronted Peter so boldly.

The Jewish party had apparently been aggressive to the point of rudeness. They came into Gentile territory, where Paul's theology was popular,
and took a public stand against him. When Peter allowed himself to be in-
timidated by that kind of rudeness, Paul confronted him. Had he not done
so, his entire ministry to the Gentiles would have been in jeopardy.

If the Jewish party was bold, Paul was more bold. He was capable of
matching them move for move, and in this instance he felt that tact was
less important than the future of the gospel to the Gentiles. I think it is safe
to say that at that moment the entire future history of Christianity was at
stake. Suppose Paul had not confronted Peter at this time. Suppose he had
followed Peter's line of reasoning and joined him in not eating with Gentile
Christians. He would have undone everything he had defended for so
many years, and the history of Christianity might have been much different.

Why did Paul include this story in his letter to the Galatian believers?
Let's keep in mind his purpose. The Jewish party claimed that Paul got his
gospel from the leadership in Jerusalem. By including this story, Paul
clinched his point that church leadership was not the source of his gospel,
because one of the church's top leaders, who earlier had approved Paul's

gospel, yielded to the Jewish party's influence. Paul confronted him publicly and forced the issue to a showdown. Paul did not tell us what Peter's response was, but we can assume that he accepted Paul's rebuke and ate with Gentile Christians.

What better human confirmation of his gospel could Paul have gotten than that?

---

* See *The Seventh-day Adventist Bible Commentary*, vol. 6, pp. 318, 319, for a detailed discussion of this problem.

CHAPTER 5

How Special Are Jews?
Galatians 2:15-19

A number of years ago I belonged to an Adventist congregation that was making plans to construct a new church. Since money was not plentiful in that particular town, the question naturally arose as to how the congregation would pay for this ambitious project that was estimated to cost well in excess of $1 million. A building fund was established, and the members contributed about $150,000 a year for several years.

That would have been a lot of money for me to stick in my pocketbook, but for a church that needed considerably more than $1 million it was not nearly enough. The church had already sold its old facility and was renting from another denomination to the tune of nearly $1,000 a month. Even at a zero inflation rate, nobody was eager to spend the next eight years ($150,000 x 8 = $1,200,000) raising the money. And given the realities of inflation and interest on a loan, at $150,000 a year the church was probably looking at 15 or 16 years to finance the project. The church's leadership decided that something had to be done to increase the level of giving.

I was a member of the board at the time, and we discussed a variety of possibilities. The options finally came down to just two: use a fund-raising program that had been devised in another conference and implemented there with some success, or retain a professional church fund-raising organization to assist us. The board voted to fly in representatives from both the other conference and from a professional fund-raising organization to make presentations. The conference-sponsored project was, of course, Seventh-day Adventist. The gentleman who made the presentation on behalf of the professional church fund-raising organization was a member of the Baptist Church, as I recall, but his organization was not affiliated with any denomination.

Naturally there were strong supporters on the board for each method of fund-raising, and also strong objections. The two strongest objections against retaining the professional fund-raising organization were (1) that it would cost a little more than $40,000 in fees and expenses, and (2) that we should not have to go to non-Adventists for advice on how to do the Lord's work when we have the Bible and the red books.

I am happy to tell you that the church retained the professional fund-raising organization and in three years raised about $750,000. I am not so happy to tell you that some members of the congregation felt so strongly that it was a mistake to engage those whom they termed "Philistines" to assist with our spiritual work that they joined another Adventist church family in the area.

Personally, I feel highly offended anytime I hear an Adventist refer to Christians of other denominations as "Philistines." There are wonderful Christian people in every denomination, and the Lord loves them and is just as eager to save them in His kingdom as He is to save you and me. And, believe it or not, sometimes the Lord can use these Christians of other faiths to help us in our ministry. Sometimes they can help us grow spiritually! In spite of what some of us may think, *Adventists do not have a corner on heaven.*

I am comforted by one thought, though: Religious prejudice is nothing new among Christians. We've seen this already in the historical part of Galatians—Jewish Christians who could not tolerate Gentile Christians. The last half of Galatians 2 gets us into the theological part of the book, and it reveals the same deep-seated prejudices.

Let's begin our study of the last half of Galatians 2 by reading the verses we will be examining: "We who are Jews by birth and not 'Gentile sinners' know that a man is not justified by observing the law, but by faith in Jesus Christ. So we, too, have put our faith in Christ Jesus that we may be justified by faith in Christ and not by observing the law, because by observing the law no one will be justified. If, while we seek to be justified in Christ, it becomes evident that we ourselves are sinners, does that mean that Christ promotes sin? Absolutely not! If I rebuild what I destroyed, I prove that I am a lawbreaker. For through the law I died to the law so that I might live for God" (verses 15-17).

Notice Paul's opening words in this statement: "We who are Jews by birth." We can assume that, as with most of the churches Paul raised up, the Galatian congregation was a mixture of Jewish and Gentile Christians. It's obvious that when Paul said, "We who are Jews by birth," he was addressing only the Jewish contingent in the church and not the entire congregation. Furthermore, his use of the pronoun *we* makes it clear that, at least for the sake of the present argument, he was identifying himself with the Jewish side of the congregation. And apparently the percentage of Jews in the Galatian churches was quite high. When we come to chapter 3 we will discover that Paul went to great lengths to explain to the Galatian Christians the meaning of the Old Testament legal system. That would hardly have been necessary in a letter to a congregation made up mostly of Gentiles, because Gentiles would not have been that interested in the Old Testament legal system.*

Let's continue with that first sentence in verse 15: "We who are Jews by birth *and not 'Gentile sinners.'"* Who were these "Gentile sinners" Paul referred to? Was he talking about born-again Gentile Christians or unconverted pagans? I think he had in mind Gentiles in their unconverted state. If this is true, then Paul was contrasting natural-born Jews with natural-born Gentiles—both in their unconverted state, both equally unsaved before God. However, think carefully about Paul's words. "We who are Jews by birth and not 'Gentile sinners'" suggests that Jews were somehow better than Gentiles, even in their unconverted state.

"But that doesn't sound like Paul," you say. "Paul taught that everyone started out equally sinful before God."

Exactly. So why did he make it sound, in this instance, as though Jews were somehow better than Gentiles? I would like to suggest that the expression "Gentile sinners" did not originate with Paul, but rather with the Jewish party. In the context of the racial tensions of the times, the expression "Gentile sinners" probably sounded about as welcome to Gentile ears back then as the word "nigger" does to Black Americans today—as welcome as "Philistines" sounds to me in reference to Christians of other faiths. So why did Paul speak of "Gentile sinners"? Not, I suspect, because he believed what the term implied, but because he was responding to an argument of the Jewish party. The NIV suggests this by putting the words *Gentile sinners* in quotation marks.

Let's read Galatians 2:15, 16 again, and please pay careful attention, because we're headed into deep water: "We who are Jews by birth and not 'Gentile sinners' know that a man is not justified by observing the law, but by faith in Jesus Christ. So we, too, have put our faith in Christ Jesus that we may be justified by faith in Christ and not by observing the law, because by observing the law no one will be justified."

Notice that Paul is back to his old theme of justification by faith and not by works of the law. This was the dominant theme of his entire ministry. The puzzling thing is how he said it in this particular instance. He began by pointing out that Jewish Christians were already well aware of the fact that a person is saved by faith and not by observing the law. He said, "We who are Jews by birth . . . know that a man is not justified by observing the law."

We would expect him to follow that up by saying, "When Gentiles put their faith in Christ, *they* are *also* justified by faith and not by works of the law." But Paul turned that around and instead said, "So we, too [that is, we Jewish Christians], have put our faith in Christ Jesus that *we* may be justified by faith in Christ and not by observing the law." Instead of saying "Gentiles who believe are saved," Paul said, "We Jews who believe are saved."

The point here is subtle, but crucial. Perhaps a diagram will help make it more clear:

WHAT WE WOULD EXPECT PAUL TO HAVE SAID	
Proposition 1	**Proposition 2**
We Jews already know that we are saved by faith and not by works of the law.	The same is true of Gentiles. *They* are saved by faith just like we Jews, when they put their faith in Christ Jesus.

Notice the italicized word "they" under proposition 2. It suggests that Gentiles are saved the same way Jews are—by faith. That sounds like good Pauline theology, doesn't it? But that's not what Paul said. The next diagram outlines his reasoning the way he actually said it:

WHAT PAUL ACTUALLY SAID	
Proposition 1	**Proposition 2**
We Jews already know that we are saved by faith and not by works of the law.	So *we, too* [Jewish Christians], have put our faith in Christ Jesus, that we may be justified by faith in Christ.

The key words here are "we, too." The Revised Standard Version, the *New American Standard Bible*, and the New King James Version all say,

"*Even we* have believed in Christ Jesus." Whether it's "we, too" or "even we," the implication is the same. Paul was not saying "Gentiles are saved like we Jews." He said exactly the opposite—"We Jews are saved like Gentiles."

During my initial in-depth study of Galatians, I puzzled for the longest time over this apparent inversion in logic. It seemed to me that the whole point of Paul's contention with the Jewish party was that Gentiles could be saved by faith just as much as Jews. Why, then, did he say "We Jews, who already know about justification by faith, have put our faith in Christ, so that *we too* might be justified by faith"? It would seem more appropriate for him to have said, "We Jews already know about justification by faith. When Gentiles put their faith in Christ, *they too* can be justified by faith."

I began to find the solution to this puzzle when I ran across the same apparently inverted logic in Acts 15. You will recall that Acts 15 tells the story of the Jerusalem Council, during which Paul and the Jewish party met head-on to determine once and for all the conditions Gentiles would have to meet in order to become Christians. Peter concluded his speech before the delegates by saying, "Now then, why do you try to test God by putting on the necks of the [Gentile] disciples a yoke that neither we nor our fathers have been able to bear? No! We believe it is through the grace of our Lord Jesus that *we* are saved, just as *they* are" (Acts 15:10, 11).

Again we see the same apparently inverted logic. Why didn't Peter say "We believe it is through the grace of our Lord Jesus that *they* are saved, just as *we* are"?

The first point I would call to your attention is that in both instances where this apparently inverted logic shows up in the New Testament, the context is the conflict with the Jewish party. I believe that both Peter and Paul were responding to an argument by the Jewish party that is never stated explicitly in the New Testament. If we had that "epistle to the Galatians" by a member of the Jewish party, I suspect we would discover that Paul's logic was not inverted at all, nor was Peter's. Since we don't have that epistle, we'll have to make do with what Paul and Peter said.

I think the Jewish party reasoned something like this: "Both Jews and Gentiles begin life as non-Christians, but we Jews have an advantage over Gentiles because of our ancestry. We have a head start on being saved." The Jewish party no doubt agreed that Jews began life as sinners too, but Jewish babies were not quite as sinful, even in their unconverted state, as unconverted Gentile babies. Somehow, their Jewishness put them a jump ahead of everyone else toward being saved.

But if being Jewish gave people a head start toward salvation, how could Gentiles be saved at all? "Ah," said the Jewish party, "by converting to Judaism. Gentiles who convert to Judaism acquire the same head start as natural born Jews. Now they are qualified to receive justification by faith." As far as the Jewish party was concerned, only Jews qualified for receiving justification by faith. Non-Jews need not apply *unless* they were prepared to become Jews first through circumcision.

That, I think, was the argument of the Jewish party. It explains the apparently inverted logic that both Peter and Paul used in responding to the Jewish party. "We Jews already know that a man is justified by faith, not by works," Peter and Paul said. "Ancestry gives the Jew no advantage, no head start whatsoever toward salvation. *We Jews are saved just like Gentiles.*"

Perhaps we can appreciate the Jewish party's deep concern a little better if we remember the background to it, which I mentioned in chapter 1 of this book. They believed that the kingdom would eventually be restored to Israel, and that at the end of time, when God established His eternal kingdom, all the world would look to Israel as the spiritual leader among the nations. But how could Israel be the great spiritual leader, the Jewish party reasoned, if Gentiles could become Christians without becoming Jews first? And how could Gentiles become Jews unless they submitted to circumcision and kept all the other laws taught by Moses? *As far as the Jewish party was concerned, Paul's theology denied everything the Old Testament stood for.* No wonder they opposed him so fiercely!

Paul's response was that every human being, Jew or Gentile, starts out before God on exactly the same footing: as sinners. Ancestry gave Jews absolutely no advantage whatsoever before God. They needed justification by faith just as much as the worst Gentile sinner. (Paul spent the first two and a half chapters of Romans elaborating on that point.) Whereas the Jewish party was saying, "Gentiles need to become more like Jews in order to be saved," Paul said, "Jews need to become more like Gentiles in order to be saved." And that must have burned the Jewish party like fire. To think that Jews would have to lower themselves to become like "those Gentile sinners" in order to be saved! The whole idea was appalling and utterly reprehensible to them.

The explanation I have given of the Jewish party's line of reasoning becomes even more clear when we read Galatians 2:17: "If, while we seek to be justified in Christ, it becomes evident that we ourselves are sinners, does that mean that Christ promotes sin?"

To put it in plain English, Paul said to the Jewish party, "So you think that we Jews have a head start on salvation because of our ancestry and that Gentiles have to avail themselves of our head start in order that *they* can be saved? I have news for you. *We* have to become sinners like them before *we* can be saved."

"Paul," the Jewish party protested, "that's terrible! If when we come to Christ we Jews are even more sinful than we were at birth, then Christ is an agent of sin. Instead of doing away with sin, by your reasoning He promotes it, at least among Jews."

That, I think, is the meaning of Paul's words in verse 17: "If, while we seek to be justified by Christ, it becomes evident that we ourselves are sinners, does that mean that Christ promotes sin?"

In the phrase "It becomes evident that we are sinners," the word *we* is in an emphatic form in the Greek, which is why the NIV translates it, "It becomes evident that we *ourselves* are sinners." That is, if in the process of coming to Christ it becomes evident that *even we Jews* are sinners, does not that make Christ an agent of sin?

"Absolutely not!" Paul replied. "If I rebuild what I destroyed, I prove that I am a lawbreaker" (verses 17, 18).

What did Paul mean by saying, "If I rebuild what I destroyed"?

Perhaps the first thing to notice is that with this statement Paul left off identifying himself with the Jewish party and began speaking in his own right. He stopped saying "we" and started saying "I."

Paul's ministry was built on establishing faith in Christ as the only source of eternal life for either Jew or Gentile, and in order to accomplish that he had to destroy the Jewish legal system as an aid in any sense to obtaining salvation. Had Paul yielded an inch of ground to the Jewish party on this point, he would have rebuilt the very method for salvation that he was trying to destroy. By that act he would have proved himself a sinner, for while the law cannot save, it can point out sin. The very law the Jewish party wanted Paul to rebuild condemned them as deserving of eternal death. And Paul said, "I can't do that. I can't rebuild what I've destroyed."

Rather, he said, "Through the law I died to the law" (verse 19). By this he probably meant that the law pointed out sin, which "killed" him and left him "dead."

I would like to conclude this chapter with two points. First, I'd like to summarize what I consider to be the real issue in Galatians. Doing that here will help us understand better some of the problems we will encounter in chapter 3. The law and circumcision were the focal points of the argument for the Jewish party, but the real issue for Paul went far beyond that. The real issue in this bitter New Testament conflict over the law was Judaism versus Christianity. The Jewish party was not arguing so much for the law as they were for being Jewish. It's just that the law is what made one Jewish. The Jewish party claimed that when Paul destroyed the law, he destroyed Jewishness. He destroyed the Jews as God's favorite people. He destroyed the promises to Abraham that the Jews would be the greatest nation in the world. He destroyed the promise to David that through his line of descent the Messiah would come. He destroyed the hope that Israel would one day rule the world.

Galatians 3 is best understood in this broader context of Judaism as a religion versus Christianity as a religion, with the law as the only way to enter into the Jewish religion. In Galatians 3 Paul will explain what it really means to be Jewish.

My second point in closing is this: We Adventists have a lot to learn from Galatians that we never thought about, and especially from the Jewish party.

Like the Jews, we believe that God has called us in a special way. We believe He has called us to prepare the world for the close of probation and the second coming of Jesus. And that's dangerous. The danger is that we will take pride in the call, that we will think more about how special we are than about the work God wants us to do. The Jewish party couldn't get over how special it was to be Jewish, and as a result, they created horrendous problems for the early Christian church.

What kind of problems do you suppose we create for Christ when we take pride in how special we are and look down our noses at other Christians who don't understand "the truth" the way we do?

Some Adventists seem fascinated with trying to figure out why Christ has delayed His coming these 150 years since 1844. If there's a reason, might it be that we're still too proud of our uniqueness, so unwilling to accept other Christians as equals that we drive them away from our message instead of attracting them to it?

What did it really mean to be Jewish in Paul's day? What does it really mean to be Seventh-day Adventist today? The right answer to that question opens up tremendous opportunities for Christian service and spiritual growth. The wrong answer leaves us spiritually stunted and the world worse off than if we'd never been in it.

---

* It could perhaps be argued that Paul went into such detail because the Galatian Christians by and large were *not* Jews. However, it seems highly unlikely that the Jewish party would have made much headway in a largely Gentile congregation. Had Paul been explaining Jewish law and history to uninformed non-Jews, he would have taken a much different approach. The whole tone of his remarks in Galatians—what he said and what he left unsaid—suggests that his purpose was not to inform his readers of Jewish law and history but to help them view in a different light what they understood very well.

CHAPTER 6

Victory in Christ
Galatians 2:20, 21

From a purely theological discussion in Galatians 2:15-19, we come now to one of the most spiritually meaningful passages in the entire New Testament. It is my favorite passage in all of Paul's writings. I first learned this passage from the King James Version, and that is still my favorite, so we will study it from that version. "I am crucified with Christ," Paul said. "Nevertheless I live; yet not I, but Christ liveth in me: and the life which I now live in the flesh I live by the faith of the Son of God, who loved me, and gave himself for me" (Gal. 2:20).

For nearly 2,000 years Christians have turned to Galatians as a major source for understanding Paul's teaching about righteousness by faith. And often, especially among Protestants, there has been a tendency to focus on chapter 3, where Paul defined justification so precisely. However, I find it significant that when Paul turned from responding to the false teaching of the Jewish party and set out to define the gospel God gave to him, he touched only briefly on justification (verses 15-19) and then turned to a discussion of the life of a transformed Christian. For that's what Galatians 2:20 is all about.

Galatians 2:20 is the language of Romans 6 to 8, where Paul talked about sanctification. It is not the language of Romans 3 to 5, which is about justification.

So let's talk about sanctification.

The first thing I want you to notice is that the opening clause of Galatians 2:20 is in the passive voice: "I am crucified with Christ." I could give you quite a long lesson about the difference between the active and the passive voice, but for our purposes in this study the important point to notice is that in the passive voice the subject of the sentence is *acted upon* rather than doing the action.

The following sentence is in the active voice: "John hit the ball." Notice that the subject, John, does something to the ball. He hits it. In the passive voice you can have a grammatically complete sentence without naming the doer of the action at all. "The ball was hit" is a complete sentence without naming who hit the ball. To name the doer of the action in a passive sentence you have to add a "by" phrase: "The ball was hit *by John.*" The passive voice is especially useful when you want to call attention to what was done without naming who did it. Like when mother comes home and asks, "How did the plate get broken?" and Johnny says, "The plate was dropped," because he doesn't want to admit, "*I* dropped the plate."

In the passive voice the subject of the sentence doesn't do anything. It just sits there and lets someone or something act upon it. That's why it's called the *passive* voice. In the sentence above, the plate was acted upon. It didn't drop itself. It was dropped by Johnny. This is the point of grammar that becomes so meaningful in Paul's short sentence, "I am crucified with Christ." Notice that the doer of the action is not named.

"But the doer *is* named," you say. "Christ is the doer of the action in that sentence."

It is probably correct to say that Christ did the action, but notice that in this sentence Paul is crucified "*with* Christ," not "*by* Christ." We'll look at Paul's "with" phrase in a moment, because it is also important. But for now let's focus our attention on the first part of the sentence: "I am crucified." Paul, the receiver of the action (crucifixion), is acted upon by someone else (the crucifier).

Logically, it has to be that way. People cannot crucify themselves. Prisoners could not lie down on a cross, pick up a hammer, and nail both hands and both feet to the cross. They might nail their feet and one hand to the cross, but the second hand would have to be nailed to the cross by someone else. Crucifixion, by its very nature, was always done *to* a prisoner, not *by* a prisoner.

A comparison of a similar passage in Romans will explain why Paul used crucifixion, which is such a passive act, to explain the Christian life. In Romans 6:6 Paul said, "For we know that *our old self* was crucified with him." Notice the passive voice again. The "old self," of course, means the Christian's sinful nature. In Galatians Paul said that *he* was crucified, but in Romans he told us exactly which part of him he meant: his *sinful nature.*

That's why crucifixion, which is such a passive act, makes such an excellent example of the way Christians overcome sin. Victory over sin begins not by the prisoner wrestling to kill his own sinful nature, but by letting someone else kill it. *It is impossible for you and me, by ourselves, to kill the evil desire for sin in our nature.*

Ellen White said: "It is impossible for us, of ourselves, to escape from the pit of sin in which we are sunken. Our hearts are evil, and we cannot change them. . . . Education, culture, the exercise of the will, human effort, all have their proper sphere, but here they are powerless. They may produce an outward correctness of behavior, but they cannot change the heart; they cannot purify the springs of life. There must be a power working from within, a new life from above, before men can be changed from sin to holiness. That power is Christ. His grace alone can quicken the lifeless faculties of the soul, and attract it to God, to holiness.

"The Saviour said, 'Except a man be born from above,' unless he shall receive a new heart, new desires, purposes, and motives, leading to a new life, 'he cannot see the kingdom of God'" (*Steps to Christ*, p. 18).

We cannot change ourselves. We can only submit to being changed. Notice that last phrase: "Unless he shall *receive* a new heart, new desires, purposes, and motives, leading to a new life . . ." By its very nature, receiving is a passive act. Someone has to give it to us in order for us to receive it.

And it's the changed heart that we have to receive, because we cannot change our own hearts. We cannot kill our old sinful desires, and we cannot implant the new desires of Christ's kingdom. Only Jesus can kill our old evil desires, and only Jesus can implant new ones that are in harmony with His law.

Let's put Romans and Galatians together. Paul said, "My old sinful nature is crucified with Christ." He did not kill his own sinful nature, his own evil desires. He allowed Christ to do that for him. He could only receive the crucifixion. As I pointed out earlier, a prisoner could not crucify himself. Back when execution by crucifixion was practiced, many prisoners struggled mightily, and the soldiers had to force them onto the cross. However, that's not the way it was with Jesus. He lay down on the cross and put forth no resistance when He was crucified. That is a model for you and me. Christ will not force our old sinful nature to be crucified. If it is done for us at all, we must "lie down" on the cross and submit willingly to the execution.

Let's go now to the last two words in that sentence. Paul said, "I am crucified *with* Christ." What does it mean to be crucified "with Christ"?

One of the clearest teachings of the New Testament is that human beings have all acted corporately in Adam and Christ. In Romans 5:12 Paul said that "sin entered the world through one man [Adam], and death through sin, and in this way death came to all men, because all sinned." In the same way, Christ's death on the cross was for all humans: "How much more did God's grace and the gift that came by the grace of the one man, Jesus Christ, overflow to the many" (verse 15). In 2 Corinthians 5:14 Paul said, "One died for all, *and therefore all died.*"

In Galatians 2:20 Paul did not mean that he was literally on the cross with Jesus. Everyone knows that would have been historical nonsense. Paul meant that when Jesus died, He paid the death penalty for sin on behalf of the entire human race. Therefore, even though the entire human race was not physically on the cross with Jesus, God counts it as though we were "in Him," "with Him." Thus, when Christ died on the cross, legally you and I also died on the cross.

That means two things. First, it means that Jesus paid the death penalty for our sins on the cross, and therefore we don't have to pay that penalty ourselves. That's where Christ's death on the cross affects us through justification. God can forgive us and treat us as though we hadn't done anything bad whatsoever, because the penalty for our sins was paid when we died "with Jesus," "in Jesus," on the cross.

Second, Christ's death on the cross affects us through sanctification, because our old sinful nature was also on the cross with Jesus. Our old sinful nature was crucified "with Christ," opening the way for Christ to implant new desires and motives in our hearts, leading to a new life of victory over sin.

Paul went on to explain how these new motives are implanted, how we receive the new life of victory in Christ. "I am crucified with Christ," he says. *"Nevertheless I live."* Just as Christ was crucified and then came to life, so the Christian's old sinful nature is crucified so that the Christian himself can rise to a new life of victory. Paul taught exactly the same lesson in Romans 6 through the analogy of baptism: "Don't you know that all of us who were baptized into Christ Jesus were baptized into his death? We were therefore buried with him through baptism into death in order that, just as Christ was raised from the dead through the glory of the Father, we too may live a new life" (Rom. 6:3, 4).

A few verses later Paul said, "If we died with Christ, we believe that we will also live with him." And then he went on to apply this resurrection principle to our own victory over sin: "For we know that since Christ was raised from the dead, he cannot die again; death no longer has mastery over him. The death he died, he died to sin once for all; but the life he lives, he lives to God. *In the same way, count yourselves dead to sin but alive to God in Christ Jesus. Therefore do not let sin reign in your mortal body so that you obey its evil desires"* (verses 8-12).

Let's get back to Galatians 2:20. "I am crucified with Christ: nevertheless I live; *yet not I, but Christ liveth in me."*

When Paul's "old man"—when his sinful nature—died, it stayed dead. That's why he said, "I live; *yet not I, but Christ liveth in me."* Paul's old sinful nature never came back to life. Instead, Jesus Christ came to live "in him." With the old sinful desires dead, Jesus was now free to implant new desires and motives in Paul's heart. Therefore, Paul could say, "And the life which I now live in the flesh I live by the faith of the Son of God, who loved me, and gave himself for me."

We often speak about justification by faith. I want you to notice that this text speaks about sanctification by faith. Paul has clearly been discussing the place of good works in the life of the Christian, and he concluded by saying that "the life I now live in the flesh [the good works that I produce in this body of mine] *I live by the faith of the Son of God."* Faith in Jesus provides our justification—our pardon from sin. And faith in Jesus provides our sanctification—our victory over sin. As I understand it, these two combined, justification by faith and sanctification by faith, constitute righteousness by faith.

Paul concludes the second chapter of Galatians by saying, "I do not set aside the grace of God, for if righteousness could be gained through the law, Christ died for nothing!" (verse 21).

Neither justification nor sanctification can be obtained through obedience to the law. Both are gained only through faith in Jesus Christ. We can never live a "good enough" life to merit pardon, nor can we ever bring forth good deeds from a pure heart on our own. Justification requires faith in Christ's pardon for our sins, and sanctification requires faith in His transformation of our hearts. "If righteousness [whether justification or sanctification] could be gained through the law, Christ died for nothing."

We will study sanctification by faith in even greater detail in the next chapter.

CHAPTER 7

Sanctification Is by Faith Too
Galatians 3:1-5

My wife's grandmother was a real stickler for keeping the Sabbath. She wouldn't so much as boil a potato on the stove or bake it in the oven, because the Bible said, "Bake what you want to bake and boil what you want to boil" on Friday, and "save whatever is left and keep it until morning"—the Sabbath (Ex. 16:23).

However, Grandma never hesitated to come home from church on Sabbath, slice the potatoes she'd boiled the day before, and *fry* them, because the Bible didn't say you couldn't fry on the Sabbath day!

You and I smile at such extreme literalism. Unfortunately, Grandma's attitude, also known as legalism, is very much alive and well in contemporary Adventism. We've all known at least one person who's the self-appointed guardian of the church's integrity. I had a parishioner like that in a church I used to pastor. She could put the sweetest smile on her face, twinkle her eyes, and tell you exactly what you'd just done that was wrong. I'm sure she won't perish in the lake of fire for failure to sound the trumpet in Zion and warn her fellow Christians of their sins!

If you read Galatians 3:1-5 carefully, you will discover that this is exactly the problem Paul had to deal with.

Paul began Galatians 3 in an interesting way to say the least. "You foolish Galatians!" he charged, "who has bewitched you? Before your very eyes Jesus Christ was clearly portrayed as crucified" (verse 1). That's strong language! How would you like someone to confront you that way about your cherished doctrinal beliefs?

Why did Paul speak so harshly? Because he felt deeply concerned about the spirituality of his Galatian friends. In Galatians 2:20 he had said, "I am crucified with Christ." Now he said, "Before your very eyes Jesus Christ was clearly portrayed as crucified." *Christ crucified is a spiritual issue,* and the theology of the Jewish party that was making the rounds in Galatia was about to destroy that. No wonder Paul got so worked up!

In verse 2 Paul said, "I would like to learn just one thing from you:

Did you receive the Spirit by observing the law, or by believing what you heard?" He repeated the question in verse 3: "Are you so foolish? After beginning with the Spirit, are you now trying to attain your goal by human effort?" And in verse 5 he said, "Does God give you his Spirit and work miracles among you because you observe the law, or because you believe what you heard?"

Receiving the Spirit is a deeply spiritual matter.

I think it's safe to say that most Seventh-day Adventists believe in justification by faith. At least we claim to. Justification means that when we confess our sins God forgives them and declares us to be righteous. He accepts us, as Ellen White puts it, just as if we had not sinned (see *Steps to Christ,* p. 62). Our record in heaven is wiped clean, and as far as God is concerned it's as though we had never done all those sins of the past. This is an instantaneous work. That's *justification.*

However, in Galatians 3:1-5, which we are studying at the moment, Paul's focus was not justification, but the Holy Spirit. Most of us are accustomed to the idea that we receive justification by faith, but notice that Paul said Christians also receive the Spirit by faith:

- "Did you receive the Spirit by observing the law, or by believing what you heard?" (verse 2).
- "Does God give you his Spirit and work miracles among you because you observe the law, or because you believe what you heard?" (verse 5).

The Holy Spirit has a role in both justification and sanctification. We confess and seek forgiveness—justification—because we have been convicted of our sins by the Holy Spirit. That same conviction leads us to want to overcome our sins. Again the Holy Spirit comes to our rescue. He transforms our hearts, removing the desire for sin, and He gives us the power to resist temptation. That's sanctification. I would like to suggest that sanctification, just as much as justification, requires faith.

So Paul's real question to the Galatian Christians was What makes a genuine, Spirit-filled Christian? What makes a victorious Christian? Is it doing or believing? Is real religion a heart that has been transformed by the Holy Spirit, or is it lifestyle? In one sense these two cannot be separated, because our works give evidence that we have accepted the Holy Spirit by faith and have experienced a transformation of heart. The problem comes when those who do not have the transformed heart think that because they live by the rules of the lifestyle they are genuine Christians. That's legalism.

For years Seventh-day Adventists have been called legalists because we keep the seventh-day Sabbath. I don't think that is what makes us legalistic at all. There is no question that there are many legalistic Adventists, and there's no question that many (if not most) legalistic Adventists keep the Sabbath legalistically. But the Sabbath itself is not what makes them legalists. It's their whole emphasis on lifestyle. Legalism is the belief that what you do makes you religious and saves you, and anyone is in great danger of legalism whose religion puts a major emphasis on lifestyle, as Seventh-day Adventists do. In addition to rules for Sabbathkeeping, we have health reform, a dress code for adornment, and prohibitions against certain forms of entertainment.

Because Sabbathkeeping is one of our lifestyle issues, let's use it as an example for a moment.

Is it OK to wade in the water at the seaside on Sabbath afternoon, or perhaps in a river or lake near your home? You just take off your shoes and let the water wash up on your feet. I hardly think any of us would say that that's wrong. But suppose you let the water come up to your ankles. Is that wrong? How about up to your knees? Or you pull up your dress or your pant legs and let the water come up to your thighs? You even get your clothes a little wet. Is it OK to wade in the water on Sabbath as long as your clothes don't get wet?

"Well, maybe it's OK up to the thighs," you say. But suppose you get your whole body in the water and dunk your head under the surface. Then you start swimming around a bit. Is that bad? Suppose you swim across the lake. Is that worse than your neighbor who hikes around the lake on Sabbath?

I'm sure that in any group of a dozen Adventists we would find a variety of answers to these questions. The point is that these are the kinds of questions people who have a strict lifestyle start debating. Arguments like this can go on endlessly, until we realize that we're not talking about matters of faith at all. We're talking about obedience to rules and standards. The first thing you know, we're asking whether a person who swims across the lake on Sabbath afternoon is saved, whether the person who wears a little jewelry or who goes to a theater now and then is saved. And suddenly the Jewish party's line of reasoning begins to sound familiar!

Let me assure you that the Jewish party would have felt quite comfortable in some Adventist circles. They would have found great satisfaction in debating whether people who wear wedding bands and earrings or who attend the theater can be saved. I'm not saying that these issues are irrelevant. But the wearing or not wearing of jewelry is not the real issue. Attendance at theaters is not the real issue. The real issue is the mind—Am I vain? Am I proud? Do I love to feed my mind with violence and lust? It *is* appropriate to ask whether vanity and pride and debauchery threaten our salvation. If jewelry leads to vanity and pride, it's wrong. If the movies and TV programs fill our minds with spiritual trash, it's wrong. And those issues *can* very much threaten our eternal life.

Salvation has to do with the mind and who controls the mind. It has to do with the feelings that control our minds. It has to do with the Spirit and belief and faith, and not with whether you and I wade in the water up to our ankles or up to our knees or up to our thighs on the Sabbath.

"You foolish Seventh-day Adventists!" Paul would say. "Did you receive the Spirit by keeping the standards of the church, or by believing what you heard?" I fear that many of us in the Adventist Church need to listen to Paul's words to the Galatians, for one of our great temptations is to label anyone in the church who is not living the lifestyle quite the way we would an unfaithful Christian. Careful attention to what we eat and drink and wear and where we go for our entertainment have their place, but we are terribly in danger of losing out on eternal life if we take comfort in our conformance to these things as an assurance of our standing with God. Such rules have nothing to do with our standing before God. Our standing with God is our faith in Jesus Christ.

Do you feel tempted to accuse me of destroying Adventism? Then maybe you can understand the concern of the Jewish Christians who said, "Paul, you are destroying Judaism." For just as certain practices had become an important part of Judaism, so certain practices have become an important part of Adventism. And there is always the temptation to think, as the Jewish Christians did, that viewing the practices from a new (nontraditional) perspective means destroying our religion, our spirituality, and our connection with God.

We may think fellow Christians who don't live the lifestyle quite the way we do are endangering their spirituality, but we have no idea what their spiritual life is like or their connection with Christ. We simply cannot judge each other on that level. The minute we do so, we are into legalism.

Let's return now to the theme of this chapter and the theme of Paul's remarks in Galatians 3:1-5. Paul's usual question was whether a Christian received *justification* by faith or by works, but the key issue in this passage is whether Christians receive *the Holy Spirit* by faith or by works. Jesus said that the Holy Spirit is the one who converts us (see John 3:3, 5), and conversion transforms the heart, making obedience to God's law possible. Converted persons, those who have received the Holy Spirit, don't feel like they *have* to obey God's law. They *want* to obey.

So conversion and sanctification both come by faith, just as much as justification. And in the context of Paul's argument in Galatians, it is clear that conversion and sanctification have their beginning at the moment we first place our faith in Jesus Christ, just like justification.

There's somewhat of a debate in Adventism today over whether conversion is part of justification. Some people insist that justification is exclusively a legal transaction that takes place on the record books of heaven when Christ forgives a Christian's sins and that it has nothing to do with his or her internal experience. I disagree, and I believe that in Galatians 3:1-5 Paul disagrees. A respected Bible scholar who is a specialist on Galatians made the following comment about this passage:

> "Paul takes it for granted that Abraham's being justified by faith *proves* that the Galatians must have received the Spirit by faith also; and this argument from Scripture falls to the ground *unless* the reception of the Spirit is in some sense equated with justification. For if this were not so, it could be objected that even though Abraham was indeed justified by faith, it does not necessarily follow that reception of the Spirit also has to be dependent on faith; conceivably while justification is by faith the gift of the Spirit could be conditioned on works. We may take it, then, that Paul conceives of receiving the Spirit in such close connection with justification that the two can be regarded in some sense as synonymous, so that in the Galatians' receiving the Spirit their justification was also involved.
>
> "Thus, just as in the previous passage (Gal. 2:15-21) Paul interpreted his own conversion experience in terms of justification by faith, so also in the present passage (Gal. 3:1-6) the Galatians' initiatory experience of receiving the Spirit is regarded as at least involving justification by faith,

if not being totally synonymous with it. This again shows that to Paul justification stands at the inception of the Christian life as an integral part of the Christian experience" (Ronald Y. K. Fung, *The New International Commentary on the New Testament: The Epistle to the Galatians*, ed. F. F. Bruce [Grand Rapids: Eerdmans, 1988], pp. 136, 137).

My personal opinion in all this debate over justification and conversion that's making the rounds in the Adventist Church is that a lot of it has to do with theological hairsplitting that the average man or woman in the pew couldn't care less about. For the purpose of theological definitions it is important to keep conversion and justification separate, but we must understand that both begin at the first moment of faith, and both touch the heart as well as the record books of heaven. And, as Paul so clearly stated in Galatians 3:1-5, our reception of the Holy Spirit, which is the basis of conversion and sanctification, is no more based on works than is justification. Both come to us through faith and faith alone, exactly the way we receive justification.

From beginning to end, we cannot boast that we have done anything to deserve the least part of our Christian life. Everything is based on Jesus Christ and Him crucified.

That's the message of Galatians 3:1-5.

CHAPTER 3

Proving His Gospel From Scripture
Galatians 3:6-14

The Jewish party had carefully thought through their theology from Scripture. Their doctrine was thoroughly based on the Old Testament. This much seems clear from their assertion at the Jerusalem Council that "the Gentiles must be circumcised and required to obey the law of Moses" (Acts 15:5). They knew exactly what those laws were. They also knew about God's promise to make of Abraham a great nation, and they knew about His promise that the Messiah would be a descendant of David.

Up to this point in Galatians Paul has shared with us his understanding of the gospel without trying to prove it from the Bible. You and I can accept that since we know that Paul was one of the authors of the Bible. But the Jewish party did not accept Paul as a Bible writer, and Paul knew that the Jewish Christians in Galatia would demand more evidence from him than his simple claim that "God gave me my gospel by a revelation." He would have to demonstrate his gospel from Scripture. And that's what he did in Galatians 3:6-14. In these few verses he rattles off one Old Testament passage after the other. His quotations come so thick and fast that it's easy to feel confused. However, when we carefully examine his line of reasoning, it's really quite logical, and simple enough to understand.

Let's begin by quoting Galatians 3:6-14. I will italicize Paul's Old Testament quotes so that you can recognize them more easily.

"Consider Abraham: *'He believed God, and it was credited to him as righteousness.'* Understand, then, that those who believe are children of Abraham. The Scripture foresaw that God would justify the Gentiles by faith, and announced the gospel in advance to Abraham: *'All nations will be blessed through you.'* So those who have faith are blessed along with Abraham, the man of faith.

"All who rely on observing the law are under a curse, for it is written: *'Cursed is everyone who does not continue to do everything written in the Book of the Law.'* Clearly no one is justified before God by the law, because, *'The righteous will live by faith.'* The law is not based on faith; on the contrary, *'The man who does these things will live by them.'* Christ redeemed us from the curse of the law by becoming a curse for us, for it is written: *'Cursed is everyone who is hung on a tree.'* He redeemed us in order that the blessing given to Abraham might come to the Gentiles through Christ Jesus, so that by faith we might receive the promise of the Spirit."

You will probably find it easier to follow my explanation of this passage if you keep referring to it as you read. Also, since Galatians is only a summary of ideas that Paul developed at much greater length in Romans 3 and 4, in some instances we will turn to Romans for a better understanding of what Paul meant in Galatians.

Anyone who has studied Paul's writings even briefly knows that the theme of his doctrine was justification by faith apart from works of the law. And in Galatians that's the point where he began to prove his gospel from the Old Testament. "Consider Abraham," he said. " 'He believed God, and it was credited to him as righteousness.' Understand, then, that those who believe are children of Abraham." Paul quoted this verse almost word for word from Genesis 15:6: "[Abram] believed the Lord, and he credited it to him as righteousness."

In Galatians Paul commented only briefly on this passage from Genesis, but in Romans he elaborated on it in great detail. We'll understand Paul's reasoning in Galatians much better if we spend a bit of time in Romans. I will begin by quoting Romans 4:1-3: "What then shall we say that Abraham, our forefather, discovered in this matter? If, in fact, Abraham was justified by works, he had something to boast about—but not before God. What does the Scripture say? 'Abraham believed God, and it was credited to him as righteousness.' "

Notice that Paul began this passage by bringing up the possibility that Abraham might have been justified by works, but he immediately knocked that idea down by quoting the same verse from Genesis that we just read in Galatians: "Abraham believed God, and it was credited to him as righteousness." And in Romans he began by saying: "Is this blessedness only for the circumcised, or also for the uncircumcised? We have been saying that Abraham's faith was credited to him as righteousness. Under what circumstances was it credited? Was it after he was circumcised, or before? It was not after, but before! And he received the sign of circumcision, a seal of the righteousness that he had by faith while he was still uncircumcised. So then, he is the father of all who believe but have not been circumcised, in order that righteousness might be credited to them. And he is also the father of the circumcised who not only are circumcised but who also walk in the footsteps of the faith that our father Abraham had before he was circumcised" (verses 9-12).

If you never heard Paul's argument before, reading it in this passage without any explanation may leave you feeling a bit confused. However, his line of reasoning is really quite simple.

Genesis 15:6 says that "Abram believed the Lord, and he credited it to him as righteousness." However, we have to wait until we come to Genesis 17:9, 10 to read about circumcision: "Then God said to Abraham, 'As for you, you must keep my covenant, you and your descendants after you for the generations to come. This is my covenant with you and your descendants after you, the covenant you are to keep: Every male among you shall be circumcised.'" A careful examination of the biblical chronology in these chapters of Genesis shows that God credited Abraham's faith to him as righteousness (he was justified by faith) a full 17 years before He commanded Abraham to be circumcised!

The Jewish party insisted that Gentiles did not qualify to receive justification by faith *until* they were circumcised. Paul countered that argument by pointing out that the first Hebrew to be circumcised was none other than the great father of the Jewish nation, Abraham himself. And Abraham was justified by faith *before* he was circumcised. If Abraham could be justified by faith before he was circumcised, then surely Gentiles should have access to salvation without circumcision too.

That's really a simple argument, when you stop to think about it.

Paul's next "proof text" from the Old Testament also comes from Genesis. "The Scripture foresaw that God would justify the Gentiles by faith, and announced the gospel in advance to Abraham: 'All nations will be blessed through you.' So those who have faith are blessed along with Abraham, the man of faith" (Gal. 3:8, 9). According to Genesis 12:2, 3, God said to Abraham, "I will make you into a great nation and I will bless you; I will make your name great, and you will be a blessing. I will bless those who bless you, and whoever curses you I will curse; and *all peoples on earth will be blessed through you."* The italicized words are the ones Paul quoted.

With this Old Testament quotation Paul began another theme that he carried through the rest of chapter 3 and much of chapter 4. The issue is this: Who has a right to consider himself a descendant of Abraham? The Jewish party insisted that the only true descendants of Abraham were those who received the rite of circumcision, like Abraham did. But Paul said no. Anyone who believes is a descendant of Abraham.

Notice that Paul said, "The Scripture *foresaw* that God would justify the Gentiles by faith." He meant that when God said all nations would be blessed through Abraham, He actually had in mind way back then that Gentiles would be justified by faith. The gospel of justification by faith was not an afterthought. It did not originate with Jesus or Paul. It began with Abraham. Paul wrapped up his argument by saying, "So those who have faith [whether they are Jews or Gentiles] are blessed along with Abraham, the man of faith."

Up to this point Paul used the Old Testament to prove his gospel of justification by faith. Now he used the same Old Testament to show that salvation by obeying the law is impossible. "All who rely on observing the law are under a curse," he said, "for it is written: 'Cursed is everyone who does not continue to do everything written in the Book of the Law'" (Gal. 3:10). This quotation comes from Deuteronomy 27:26, which says, "Cursed is the man who does not uphold the words of this law by carrying them out."

Paul's point was that if it were possible to obey the law perfectly, then justification by works would also be possible. However, even the slightest disobedience brings a curse. And since every human being from Adam to the present has sinned (see Rom. 3:23), everyone is under its curse. Everyone is condemned to eternal death.

Paul then returned momentarily to his theme of justification by faith, and he used another of his favorite Old Testament texts: "The righteous will live by faith" (Gal. 3:11). This citation comes from Habakkuk 2:4, which says, "The righteous will live by his faith."

However, Paul immediately went back to show the inadequacy of law to save: "The law is not based on faith;" he said. "On the contrary, 'The man who does these things will live by them'" (Gal. 3:12). This statement comes from Leviticus 18:5, which says, "Keep my decrees and laws, for the man who obeys them will live by them." Righteousness by works is theoretically possible, but thousands of years of sin have shown that no human being except Christ *has ever* kept the law perfectly. Therefore, from a practical standpoint the only way any human being can ever be put right with God is through faith.

So God gave us humans a law to keep and said that if we keep it perfectly it would earn us eternal life. But nobody has ever done that, which means we are all under a curse.

Can anyone be saved, then? Absolutely! "Christ redeemed us from the curse of the law by becoming a curse for us," Paul said. "For it is written: 'Cursed is everyone who is hung on a tree'" (Gal. 3:13). Paul here cites Deuteronomy 21:23, and I will quote verse 22 as well to give you the context: "If a man guilty of a capital offense is put to death and his body is hung on a tree, you must not leave his body on the tree overnight. Be sure to bury him that same day, because anyone who is hung on a tree is under God's curse."

Paul's point is utterly clear. Although Moses, the author of Deuteronomy, did not have Christ's sacrificial death in mind when he wrote this passage, Paul applied it that way. He expanded Moses' meaning. He used Moses' words as a vehicle to show that the curse of our disobedience, which should have come upon us, actually fell on Christ. Christ took our sins in order that He might give us His righteousness. Ellen White stated it beautifully in *The Desire of Ages:* "Christ was treated as we deserve, that we might be treated as He deserves. He was condemned for our sins, in which He had no share, that we might be justified by His righteousness, in which we had no share. He suffered the death which was ours, that we might receive the life which was His. 'With His stripes we are healed'" (p. 25).

Paul wrapped up his Old Testament defense of his gospel by stating once again why it is so important: "He redeemed us in order that the blessing given to Abraham might come to the Gentiles through Christ Jesus, so that by faith we might receive the promise of the Spirit" (Gal. 3:14).

Notice a couple of things about this verse. First, all of Paul's argumentation thus far in Galatians had just one purpose: to show that the blessing given to Abraham through faith is also available to Gentiles who exercise that same faith. The Jewish party was arguing strenuously that Gentiles could receive justification by faith only if they were circumcised first and kept the other laws of Moses. But Paul said no. Abraham was justified by faith before he received the rite of circumcision, and so are the Gentiles.

Second, notice that at the end of verse 14 Paul brought his argument around to sanctification again: "So that by faith we might receive the promise of the Spirit." The whole purpose of justification is to open the way for human beings to reestablish their union with Christ through the Holy Spirit. Otherwise God would be saving people legally, on the record books of heaven, without their ever experiencing a change in their characters. Probably nowhere did Paul state the relationship between faith and works more clearly than in Ephesians 2:8-10: "For it is by grace you have been saved, through faith—and this not from yourselves, it is the gift of God—not by works, so that no one can boast. For we are God's workmanship, created in Christ Jesus to do good works, which God prepared in advance for us to do."

CHAPTER 5

God Always Keeps His Promises
Galatians 3:10-18

everal years ago, when I was pastor of the Adventist church in Alvarado, Texas, the conference asked me if I would be interested in transferring to a larger church in Waco. The change would require that my wife and I sell our house in Keene, near Alvarado. After talking it over and praying about it, we decided to accept the conference's invitation. We put a sign in front of our house in Keene and advertised in the newspaper, and some time later we were sitting in a lawyer's office signing papers. I still remember taking pen in hand, writing my name on the dotted line, and then handing the pen to my wife so she could sign her name on the dotted line. We also signed papers to purchase a new home in Waco.

Until we signed the contract to sell our old house, it was still ours. After that it belonged to someone else. Similarly, once we signed the contract for the new house, it belonged to us and not the former owner. My wife and I could now live happily in our new home, knowing that the former owners could never walk in and say, "This is still our house. We used to live here, and you'll have to move out." Neither could my wife and I go back to our old home and walk in anytime we wanted to. We could not demand to live in that house again. That house now belonged to someone else. My wife and I signed papers, the new owners signed papers, and neither of us could change that. Once a human covenant has been duly established the legal way, it cannot be changed or set aside.

That's a good analogy of what Paul meant in Galatians 3:15: "Brothers, let me take an example from everyday life. Just as no one can set aside or add to a human covenant that has been duly established, so it is in this case."

Paul was making a specific point here. He meant that once God gave salvation by faith to Abraham as a promise, He could not change and demand that salvation be based on works. God's promises are just as sure as human covenants, and even more so. If even humans cannot go back on the legal documents (covenants) that they sign, surely God can't either!

That's all very well and good, you say, but God never signed any papers with Abraham.

True enough. But a signature on paper was not the usual way people made legally binding contracts in Abraham's time. You may be amused when you discover what they *did* do. Genesis 15 tells us about it.

Abraham was desperate to have a son, and he was getting a little weary of waiting for God's promise. So, as you will recall, he proposed that his servant Eliezer be his son. It was quite customary back then for a family who could not have children to make their chief servant the heir to their estate. But God said, "No, Eliezer will not be your heir. Go outside and look up at the stars. Count them if you can. That's how numerous your offspring will be. And these people will descend from a son who will come from your own body" (see Gen. 15:1-5). It's at this point that the Bible says, "Abraham believed the Lord, and he credited it to him as righteousness" (Gen. 15:6).

The promise of an heir was now settled. However, God had also promised to give Abraham the land of Canaan (see Gen. 13:14, 15), and Abraham still had a bit of doubt about that. "'O Sovereign Lord, how can I know that I will gain possession of [the land]?' So the Lord said to him, 'Bring me a heifer, a goat, and a ram, each three years old, along with a dove and a young pigeon'" (Gen. 15:8, 9).

Abraham brought all these animals together in one place, and God told him to cut each of the animals in two (except for the birds) and set the halves opposite each other with a space in between. About sundown Abraham fell sound asleep, and a "thick and dreadful darkness came over him" (verse 12). Then God said: "Know for certain that your descendants will be strangers in a country not their own, and they will be enslaved and mistreated four hundred years. But I will punish the nation they serve as slaves, and afterward they will come out with great possessions. You, however, will go to your fathers in peace and be buried at a good old age. In the fourth generation your descendants will come back here, for the sin of the Amorites has not yet reached its full measure" (verses 13-16).

Notice that God predicted both the enslavement of the Israelites in Egypt and their return 400 years later, "in the fourth generation." (Back then a generation was significantly longer than it is today.) It was extremely important for God to inform Abraham about the Israelite captivity in Egypt ahead of time, lest after their enslavement the people should give up their faith in the promise.

But what about the "signing" of this covenant between God and Abraham? How did that happen? The Bible says that "when the sun had set and darkness had fallen, a smoking firepot with a blazing torch appeared and passed between the pieces [of the animals]" (verse 17).

In the ancient world people didn't always make their agreements legal by writing them down on a parchment and signing their names at the bottom. Instead, they would cut up some domestic animals—a heifer, a goat, or a ram—and set the pieces two or three feet apart from each other, making a path between them. The parties to the covenant then "signed" their documents by walking between those animal halves. Abraham was asleep when God "signed" the document, so he didn't walk between the animals. But God did, in the form of a smoking firepot with a blazing torch.

And that's what Paul meant in Galatians when he said, "Just as no one can set aside or add to a human covenant that has been duly established, so it is in this case." His point is that once God made certain promises to Abraham on the basis of Abraham's faith and then ratified those promises ("signed His name" to them) by passing between the halves of the animals, it was impossible for Him to go back on His word.

It's important to pay careful attention to exactly what God promised Abraham and what He did not promise him. He promised that Abraham's descendants would be as numerous as the stars in the sky and the sand in the sea (Gen. 15:5), that they would become a great nation (12:1-3), and that they would inherit the region we now call Palestine (15:7). God did *not* promise anything about salvation. He did not say to Abraham, "Believe in me, and I will give you eternal life."

However, once Abraham believed God's promise about his descendants becoming a great nation in Palestine, God credited that faith to him as righteousness. His faith in God's promise became a saving faith that led to eternal life. That's Paul's point.

You and I can experience the same blessing today. As we read through the Bible we find many promises that God has given us for help in daily living. We find help in dealing with personal problems, family problems, church problems, and job problems, to name just a few. As we believe these promises, God credits that faith to us as righteousness.

Believing that Christ died on a cross to save us from sin and that He rose the third day to give us a new life in union with Him are most assuredly included in what we call "righteousness by faith." But so is trusting

God enough to make Him Lord in all the affairs of our lives. God credits *all* our faith in Him as righteousness, including our faith in His direction over our everyday lives.

Paul went on to say that "the promises were spoken to Abraham and to his seed. The Scripture does not say 'and to seeds,' meaning many people, but 'and to your seed,' meaning one person, who is Christ" (Gal. 3:16). Christ is the promise in the most ultimate sense, because the promise would have been nothing more than empty words without Him. While God did not actually say so, Paul interpreted His promise to Abraham to mean that someday Jesus Christ would come and die on the cross and make it possible for everyone to receive righteousness by faith.

God's promises are sure. Whatever God has promised, we may claim just as if we had a signed and sealed document. But we must claim it by faith. A promise, by its very nature, requires faith on the part of the one receiving it. Once the promise has been fulfilled, faith is no longer necessary. If I promise my wife that I will bring her something from the store, she has faith to believe that I will do that. Once I walk through the door with those items in my hands, she no longer has to have faith in me. She sees the things she asked for, and she knows I bought them. But until the promise is fulfilled, the one who received it can only trust the one who gave it.

One of the most fundamental principles of life is that we must be able to trust each other. A society with no trust would be a terrible society in which to live. Every time I sign a credit card slip, I'm giving my promise to the credit card company that I will pay. Every time I pay my bill on time, I build the credit card company's trust in me. For Paul, the issue was God's trustworthiness: "The law introduced 430 years later," he said, "does not set aside the covenant previously established by God and thus do away with the promise. For if the inheritance depends on the law, then it no longer depends on a promise; but God in his grace gave it to Abraham through a promise" (verses 17, 18).

Apparently the Jewish party claimed that the law God gave on Sinai annulled the promise to Abraham. Paul kept saying "The promise, the promise, the promise . . ." and they kept saying "Yes, but the law, the law, the law. . . ." What they meant was that the law, when it came, annulled the promise that God made to Abraham. But Paul said no. A human document that has been signed and sealed cannot be changed. How much less can you change a promise—a "document"—that God "signed" for Abraham?

Paul's point was that whatever purpose the law served during the 1,500 years from Sinai to Calvary, it did not do away with righteousness by faith. It did not replace the way of salvation by the promise that was given to Abraham.

We've all no doubt had the experience of accepting a promise from someone, only to have the promise broken. The more the promise means to you, the harder it is to take when the promise is broken. We don't feel very good about broken promises, and we feel even worse toward people who break their promises. I can still remember a fellow who swindled me out of a good bit of money. He got my confidence—my faith—and then he used that confidence to swindle me. He even signed a paper saying he would pay me back, and then he didn't. You can be sure that I didn't feel very good about that man.

Now, think about how you and I would feel toward God if we thought that after promising righteousness to Abraham on the basis of faith He had broken that promise 430 years later with the law. Paul's point is that you and I can trust God. He did not break His promise to Abraham and his descendants when He gave the law 430 years later. Sinai did not annul the covenant that God "signed" when He walked between those animals.

This is a good lesson for us in trustworthiness. How reliable are we as Christians? How reliable should we be? What does the world have a right to expect from us? The answer is absolute integrity. Psalm 15:4 says that only those who swear to their own hurt and change not will have access to God's kingdom. Christians need to build that kind of reputation for themselves. This is the loving thing to do. Love is not a feeling. It's a principle that works regardless of how we may feel. If we were to go on feelings alone, it is doubtful that many of us would swear to our own hurt and change not. It's not much fun to get hurt, and it's easy for us humans to change in order to avoid getting hurt. But the right thing, and therefore the loving thing to do, is to swear to one's own hurt and refuse to change. That is one of the foundations on which love rests, and that is why God could not, would not, allow the law to void the promise He made to Abraham.

The problem in Galatia was not that the Jewish party and the Galatians were actually causing God to go back on His promise. But they were treating Him as though He had gone back on His promise, and psychologically the result is the same. If you keep a promise to me but I'm misinformed and think that you broke your promise, then to me it's the same as if you *had* broken your promise. Similarly, if we think God cannot be trusted, it's the same to us as if He really could not be trusted.

According to Paul, the good news of the gospel is not only that God can be trusted, but that trusting Him is the only way to salvation. "For God so loved the world that he gave his one and only Son, that whoever believes in him shall not perish but have eternal life" (John 3:16).

And that is a promise God will never break.

CHAPTER 10

The Gospel According to Sinai—Part 1
Galatians 3:19, 20

ur study in this chapter covers just two verses of Galatians 3, but one of them (verse 19) is crucial, because it appears to suggest that God gave the law for people in Old Testament times only. In the next chapter we will discover that Galatians 3:24, when translated exactly as it reads in the Greek, says the same thing. Thus, Galatians 3:19 and 24 have become favorite texts for those who would like us to believe that New Testament Christians are no longer obligated to keep the Ten Commandments.

If we had only Galatians to go by, we might more easily conclude that the Ten Commandments were done away with when Christ came. However, Romans makes it utterly clear that the Ten Commandments have an important function in the lives of New Testament Christians. Because Romans is so clear on this point, we are forced to go back to Galatians and look more carefully at those texts where Paul seems to say that the law was done away with when Christ came, to see if what he *appears* to say about law is what he *intended* to say. That's what we are going to do in this chapter and the one that follows.

Before going any further, let's read the passage that we will be studying in this chapter: "What, then, was the purpose of the law? It was added because of transgressions until the Seed to whom the promise referred had come. The law was put into effect through angels by a mediator. A mediator, however, does not represent just one party; but God is one" (verse 19).

In a moment we'll begin analyzing these verses, but first let's do a quick review of chapter 9 in this book.

By the time the Jewish party arrived in Galatia they had become well aware of Paul's argument that the promise of righteousness by faith was given to Abraham *before* he was circumcised. They knew that he used this fact of history to justify his acceptance of Gentiles into the Christian church without requiring them to submit to circumcision. And they were smart enough to know that they had to respond to his argument or risk losing their influence in the church. We do not have their response in writing, but from what Paul said, we can guess what it was: that the law, which came 430 years after Abraham, superseded the promise to Abraham of righteousness by faith. It was essentially the reverse of the argument we hear so often today, that the gospel of righteousness by faith did away with the Ten Commandments. The Jewish party claimed that the law at Sinai did away with the righteousness by faith promised to Abraham.

Paul argued just as strongly against this false teaching in his day as we do against the idea that the law has been abolished in our day. His response in Galatians 3:15-18, which we studied in the previous chapter of this book, was that even human contracts cannot be broken once they are signed; how much less God's promise, His contract with Abraham.

However, Paul realized that it was not enough to explain that God could not break His contract with Abraham. If the law didn't supersede the promise, then he had to explain what it *did* do. That's the point of his question in verse 19: "What, then, was the purpose of the law?"

It's important that we understand the function of this sentence in Paul's argument. One of the methods that writers use again and again is what we call "transitions." A transition may be a single word, a sentence, or an entire paragraph. A transition signals readers that the writer is shifting to another part of the argument. It tells readers, "Here's what I'm going to discuss with you next."

Paul was a skillful writer, and he used transitions like any good writer. One of the best transitions anywhere in his writings is found in the opening sentence of Galatians 3:19: "What, then, was the purpose of the law?" These words signalled the Galatian Christians that he was about to launch into an explanation of the purpose of the law as *he* understood it, in contrast to the way the *Jewish party* understood it. Paul actually continued this theme through to the end of chapter 4, and we even find some rather strong hints of it in chapter 5.

It would be easy to suppose that Paul's purpose in discussing the law in Galatians was to expose the misuse of law by some of the Pharisees, which had crept into Judaism by Christ's time. But this was not Paul's purpose. Galatians was Paul's response to the Jewish party, and it is probably safe to say that the Jewish party had abandoned the extreme misperceptions of the law as it was understood by certain Pharisees almost as much as Paul had. I suspect that if we could have heard them out, the Jewish party would have told us that their desire was to restore the *true* purpose of the law the way God intended it when He gave it at Sinai. The point is that in Galatians Paul disagreed with the Jewish party's understanding of the *true* function of the law. That's why he raised the question "What, then, was the purpose of the law?"—that is, what was the proper function of the law as God gave it at Sinai?

Before going further I'd like to point out that Paul did not ask, "What was the purpose of the Ten Commandments?" (the moral law). Nor did he ask, "What was the purpose of the tabernacle service?" (the ceremonial law). Paul had in mind the entire Sinai revelation. And, as we will notice in greater detail later, Sinai was, above all else, God's revelation of His will in terms of law. When Paul asked, "What, then, was the purpose of the law?" he had in mind moral law, ceremonial law, and any other kind of divine command—Sinai as a total package.

Having asked what was the purpose of the law, Paul wasted no time getting started with his answer. And his first words are rather startling to Seventh-day Adventists. He said, "It [the law] was added because of transgressions *until the Seed . . . had come.*" The Seed, of course, was Christ (see verse 16), which makes Paul appear to be saying that the law was put into effect until Christ came. The implication is that after Christ—after the cross—the law ceased to have any valid function. That's why this is such a favorite text of those who would like us to believe that the Ten Commandments were done away with by Christ.

I began to understand the answer to this puzzling problem when I noticed that in this verse Paul mentioned two of the greatest events in biblical history: Sinai and Calvary. It is impossible to stress too much the importance of these two revelations. Twice since the fall of Adam and Eve, God has revealed Himself *in person* to the human race, and these revelations were very different from each other. As we noted a moment ago, at Sinai God revealed Himself primarily in terms of law. Even a brief look at the last half of Exodus and the entire book of Leviticus confirms this. These books, which are a summary of God's revelation to Moses at Sinai, are primarily books of law.

In Jesus Christ, on the other hand, God revealed Himself through a Person. I think this is what John meant in chapter 1 of his Gospel: "For the law was given through Moses; grace and truth came through Jesus Christ" (John 1:17). Some people try to use this verse to prove that the law was done away with when Jesus came, but I don't think that is what John had in mind at all. He was simply saying that God's revelation of Himself at Sinai was primarily in terms of law, while His revelation through Jesus Christ was primarily in terms of grace. John did not say that Christ did away with the law.

Let's look now at another passage—this one in Romans—that will help us understand what Paul meant when he talked about law in Galatians: "What advantage, then, is there in being a Jew, or what value is there in circumcision? Much in every way! First of all, they [the Jews] have been entrusted with the very words of God" (Rom. 3:1, 2).

The way some Christians talk about the law, you'd think it was something terrible. But did God come down on Mount Sinai to burden His people with something dreadful? Does God ever give His people unfortunate gifts? Of course not. In its time, the law that God revealed at Sinai was the best He had to offer. That's why Paul could say that the Jews had a tremendous advantage over Gentiles, because "they have been entrusted with the very words of God."

Here's something else I want you to notice about both Sinai and Calvary. Each was the beginning of a new religion. Sinai began the Israelite religion. Calvary began the Christian religion. And each was God's true religion for its time.

Notice also that each of these religions replaced the system that preceded it, and each was a great improvement over the preceding system. The patriarchal system of religion that preceded Judaism centered in the family, with the father or grandfather acting as priest for the family. At Sinai God replaced the patriarchal system of religion with a national religion that had a tabernacle and a priesthood to serve the entire nation. This was a great improvement over the patriarchal religion. Similarly, Christianity, which began at Calvary, replaced Judaism and was a great improvement over Judaism.

In one sense, the patriarchal system of religion, the Jewish religion that God revealed at Sinai, and the Christian religion are the same. God did not change His plan of salvation either at Sinai or at Calvary. Christians still hold the entire Old Testament to be inspired—a document that covers both the patriarchal and the Jewish periods of history. But the outward forms of patriarchalism and Judaism changed respectively at Sinai and Calvary, and many profound insights were added. From each of these changed forms and added insights there developed a new religious culture—a new religion. Paul's whole point in Galatians is that we must not allow the forms of the previous religion to dominate our present religion.

Human beings do not remain static. Society and social structures evolve and develop and change during time. Religion is one of humanity's most important social structures, and it is important to understand that this social structure will also evolve and change throughout time. Sometimes that evolution is in the wrong direction, which is one reason God sometimes replaces one religion with another. Judaism of the first century could no longer fulfill God's purpose, which is one of the important reasons why God replaced it with Christianity. If Revelation is correct, Christianity as a whole at the end of the world will have become so imperfect that God will have to replace it with the "religion" you and I will know in heaven, after the second coming of Christ.

How God's true religion will evolve, whether patriarchalism, Judaism, or Christianity, depends a great deal on the form in which God revealed the religion at its inception. The Jewish religion grew out of God's revelation at Sinai, and since at Sinai God revealed Himself primarily in terms of law, it should come as no surprise that the Jewish religion evolved in terms of law. You will understand Galations 3:21-24 (which we will examine in chapter 11) much more easily if you keep in mind that the Jewish religion, particularly as the Israelites received it at Sinai, was God's true religion. As it evolved, it continued to be God's true religion—even when that evolution was sometimes quite imperfect—until God replaced it with Christianity.

It is also extremely important to understand that God gave the law to His people because He wanted them to have a much deeper, richer spiritual experience than they had ever had before. Perhaps you're wondering whether law can really lead to a deeper, richer religious experience. That is a hard thing for Christians to understand, because we are so used to gaining our deep religious experiences through our relationship with Jesus. But the Jews in the Old Testament didn't know the story of Jesus the way you and I do. If they were to experience revival at all, they had to experience it through the revelation they had, and the best revelation available to them was the law God gave at Sinai.

In case you question whether law can bring revival, I'd like to call your attention to an incident in the Old Testament. During the time of the kings of Judah the Temple fell into disuse for several centuries, but then somebody started cleaning out all the cobwebs and dusting off all the furniture. And what should they find in some dark corner but a book of the law. Someone brought the book of the law to the king, and the king read it to all the people, and it worked a tremendous revival (see 2 Chron. 34).

What brought about this revival? The reading of the law.

It's extremely important to understand that before Jesus died on the cross, law was not a bad thing. It was God's plan. It was the best He had to offer up to that point. When rightly used, it brought spiritual revival.

Let's return to Galatians.

When Paul asked, "What, then, was the purpose of the law?" he was asking about the purpose of the law during the Jewish period of biblical history. This is particularly evident from his next words: "It was added because of transgressions until the Seed to whom the promise referred had come."

As we noted a moment ago, whatever God's purpose for law was between Sinai and Calvary, it was very good. God never gives anything that has a bad purpose. So whatever Paul says next in Galatians, we can expect to hear him talking about the right use of law, the way God intended it when He gave it at Sinai. He will also be talking about the right use of the Jewish religion that grew out of that law.

And what did Paul say was God's purpose in giving the law at Sinai? "It was added because of transgressions."

We do have a minor problem here, though—what appears to be a blatant contradiction with something Paul said in verse 15. "No one can set aside or add to a human covenant that has been duly established," he said, and "so it is in this case." But now, in verse 19, he tells us that the law was added.

Perhaps a comparison with a minor point of modern law having to do with wills can clarify Paul's meaning.

A "codicil" is "an addition to a will to change, explain, revoke, or add provisions" (*Webster's New World Dictionary*, second college edition). In verse 15 Paul went out of his way to emphasize that no one can set aside a human covenant, and at the very least he means that the law did not *revoke* God's promise to Abraham. Also, we are probably safe in saying that it did not *change* the promise in any significant way. But it did *explain* it, and, as we shall see, it did enhance it.

There are two parts to this short sentence, and we need to examine each part separately. First, Paul said that the law "was added." What was it added to? The context will help us answer that question: "The law, introduced 430 years later, does not set aside the covenant previously established by God and thus do away with the promise. For if the inheritance depends on the law, then it no longer depends on a promise; but God in his grace gave it to Abraham through a promise. What then was the purpose of the law? It was added."

Added to what? *It was added to the promise.* When you add something, you don't do away with the thing you add it to. That would be subtraction. To add you have to take two things and put them together. The law was *added,* not subtracted. It didn't *replace* the promise. It was *put with* the promise.

Paul wanted to impress his readers with the superiority of the promise over the law, as opposed to the Jewish party, which insisted on the superiority of the law over the promise. The Jewish party taught that the law replaced the promise—or at least took preeminence over the promise. But Paul said no. The law could be *added* to the promise to explain and enhance it, but it could not *replace* the promise, or even hold a superior position over the promise.

Now for the second part of the short sentence. Why was the law added? Paul said it was added "because of transgressions." What did he mean by that? Paul made a similar statement in Romans 5:20 that helps us to understand what he meant in Galatians 3:19. He said, "The law was added *so that the trespass might increase.*" God gave the law at Sinai so that sin might appear more sinful. The law was added to the promise to bring about a greater awareness of sin.

Jesus did the same thing in the Sermon on the Mount. He pointed out that sin is a matter not just of what we do but of what we feel in our hearts. Sin is not so much whether you kill someone. It's whether you hate that person. It's not whether you commit the physical act of adultery. It's whether you look upon a person of the opposite sex with lust in your heart. Jesus did the very same thing God intended that the law should do: He made sin to appear more sinful. He probed to the depths of what sin really means and exposed it for what it really is, so that we sinful humans can more easily recognize it in our own lives.

The Holy Spirit continues to do the same thing today. In John 16:8 Jesus told His disciples that when the Holy Spirit came He would convict the world of sin. The great disease of the human family is sin, and God has to make us aware of sin before righteousness by faith can do us any good whatsoever. The awareness or conviction of sin is the starting place for salvation by faith. That's why the law was "added to" the promise. The purpose of the law was not to do away with the promise of righteousness by faith, but to enhance it by making sin appear truly sinful, so that righteousness by faith could do its work.

There is another principle I like to emphasize whenever I write or speak on this subject, and this also comes from Romans 5:20. If we had kept reading that verse a bit ago, we would have come to this principle: "The law was added so that the trespass might increase. *But where sin increased, grace increased all the more."*

I like that. Anytime God gives us a greater awareness of sin, He also gives us a greater awareness—a greater understanding—of the plan of salvation. And when you look at what happened at Sinai, that's exactly what He did. He gave the children of Israel a much deeper understanding of sin through what we call the moral law, and He followed that up with a much deeper understanding of His plan of salvation through what we know as the ceremonial law. When Jesus came He gave us a much deeper understanding of sin through His Sermon on the Mount, and through His life and death He revealed the gospel in its absolute fullness. At both Sinai and Calvary, where sin abounded, grace abounded all the more.

The same is true of the Holy Spirit. The Spirit convicts us, making us more aware of sin, and when we accept that conviction and repent of our sin, He transforms our hearts so that we no longer want to sin. Where sin abounds—wherever the revelation of sin is increased so that we understand it better—grace abounds all the more. *God never gives a greater understanding of sin without a greater understanding of the plan of salvation to go along with it.*

We who live during the Christian Era tend to think of law and grace as opposites, almost as though they fight each other. An Old Testament Jew who understood God's true purpose in giving the law would never have made that mistake. Why? Because at Sinai both morality and grace were revealed in the form of law. The Jews learned morality and grace together through law, rather than as opposites.

In the next few paragraphs I'd like to focus our attention on the ceremonial part of the law, and I want to begin by stating the principle we've been talking about: *the ceremonial law was really the gospel revealed in terms of law.*

That's why the title of this chapter and the next is "The Gospel According to Sinai." The sacrifices that the Jews offered were a type of the cross, and the ministry of the priests in the tabernacle was a type of Christ's mediatorial ministry in heaven. The Day of Atonement was a type of God's final judgment and the disposition of sin. *The people in the Old Testament found forgiveness and reconciliation with God through the ceremonial law.* If that seems hard to understand, read Leviticus 4:27-31:

> "If a member of the community sins unintentionally and does what is forbidden in any of the Lord's commands, he is guilty. When he is made aware of the sin he committed, he must bring as his offering for the sin he committed a female goat without defect. He is to lay his hand on the head of the sin offering and slaughter it at the place of the burnt offering. Then the priest is to take some of the blood with his finger and put it on the horns of the altar of burnt offering and pour out the rest of the blood at the base of the altar. He shall remove all the fat, just as the fat is removed from the fellowship offering, and the priest shall burn it on the altar as an aroma pleasing to the Lord. In this way the priest will make atonement for him [the sinner], and he will be forgiven."

Notice the end result of this ceremony: sinners were forgiven. Their sins were atoned for. That's exactly what grace does today! But back then sinners could not just say, "God, please forgive me," the way we do. They had to bring a female goat without defect to the priest, lay their hand on it, and kill the goat themselves. When the goat was dead, the priest had to dip his finger in its blood and put it on the horns of the altar of burnt offering, and he had to pour out the rest of the blood at the base of the altar. Then he had to remove all the fat and burn it on the altar. Only after all this ritual was completed could sinners consider themselves forgiven.[1]

Now I want you to notice something: this ritual, which brought the same forgiveness that you and I get through coming directly to Jesus, came to the Jews through a law. Even the priest's clothing was prescribed by this law, and every step he went through to obtain forgiveness for sinners was stated in terms of law.

How would you like to go through all that in order to get your sins forgiven? We would find this terribly cumbersome today. Yet in its time, that was grace! It was the gospel according to Sinai, revealed in terms of law, and 1,500 years before the cross it was the best God could offer. *This was God's way,* and it was a tremendous improvement over any gospel the world had ever known before. (I don't mean that God came up with a new plan of salvation at Calvary. But each time He reveals Himself to the human race, He adds to what went before, which makes the latter an improvement over the former.)

Let's examine another phase of this question. At the risk of being misunderstood, I would like to suggest that the ceremonial law was the Jews' entry point into salvation. I don't mean that the ceremonies themselves saved them. But they did introduce God's people to salvation. It was the way God provided for them to enter into the experience of salvation. We can compare it to baptism. Is baptism necessary to be saved? Of course not. In one sense baptism just washes the skin. Yet in a real sense baptism *is* necessary, because God has provided this symbolic act as a way of expressing outwardly what He has done for us inwardly. Baptism is a visible entry point for Christians into salvation. We even wait to admit people to church membership until they've been baptized.

Or consider the Lord's Supper. Is Communion necessary in order to be saved? Not in the Roman Catholic sense that the bread and wine of themselves impart God's grace. Yet we find salvation in the Communion service because the Holy Spirit is there to impart His power. Do we miss a saving experience with God when we deliberately choose to absent ourselves from the Communion service? Of course. So Communion is a symbolic act by which we enter into a closer saving relationship with God. In this sense we can think of it as an entry point into salvation. Even though the service itself doesn't save, doing it puts us into a closer relationship with God, and that relationship saves.

That, I believe, is how we need to think of the ceremonial law in Old Testament times. It was a way for the Jews to obtain the experience of salvation, and it was stated in terms of law. Unfortunately, the Jews allowed these ceremonies to degenerate into a form, so that by the time of Isaiah God had to say to them: "Hear the word of the Lord, you rulers of Sodom; listen to the law of our God, you people of Gomorrah! 'The multitude of your sacrifices—what are they to me?' says the Lord. 'I have more than enough of burnt offerings, of rams and the fat of fattened animals; I have no pleasure in the blood of bulls and lambs and goats. . . . Stop bringing meaningless offerings! Your incense is detestable to me. New Moons,

Sabbaths and convocations—I cannot bear your evil assemblies. Your New Moon festivals and your appointed feasts my soul hates. They have become a burden to me; I am weary of bearing them'" (Isa. 1:10-14).

Why did God say this, when He was the one who gave them these burnt offerings as a way to have a closer experience with Him? Because the people had allowed these rituals to degenerate into nothing more than a form, thinking that going through the motions was enough to win them God's favor. But they failed to experience the presence of the Holy Spirit in their hearts through these rituals. When the Jews truly entered into the experience of salvation through the rituals that God gave them, those rituals were a tremendous blessing. The sacrifice of the lamb was their way of receiving forgiveness. But when they observed the ceremonial law merely to gain favor with God, it was useless.

So we can say, then, that while the ceremonial law did not save the Jews, rightly used it provided a way for them to enter into a relationship with God and into the experience of forgiveness and grace. It helped them experience the gospel.

We've said a lot about the proper and improper functions of law in the Old Testament. Let's put it all on a chart:

OLD TESTAMENT	
Proper function of law	**Improper function of law**
1. As a way to learn about sin 2. As a way to learn about grace and God's plan of salvation 3. As a symbolic way to enter into the experience of salvation	1. As a way to gain favor with God

Now let's look at the New Testament. What are the proper and improper functions of law for New Testament Christians? Paul made it quite clear, especially in Romans, that one of the proper functions of law in the New Testament is to reveal sin. Let's look at some of those passages: "Now we know that whatever the law says, it says to those who are under the law, so that every mouth may be silenced and the whole world held accountable to God. Therefore no one will be declared righteous in his sight by observing the law; rather, through the law we become conscious of sin" (Rom. 3:19, 20). "What shall we say, then? Is the law sin? Certainly not! Indeed I would not have known what sin was except through the law. For I would not have known what coveting really was if the law had not said, 'Do not covet'" (Rom. 7:7). "In order that sin might be recognized as sin, it [the law] produced death in me through what was good, so that through the commandment sin might become utterly sinful" (verse 13).

These passages leave no doubt that in New Testament times the law still served as a moral guide to show God's people the difference between right and wrong. So we can put it down, then, that one of the proper functions of law in the New Testament era is to provide us with moral standards of right and wrong.

Are there any other proper functions of law in the New Testament? The ceremonial law revealed God's plan of salvation to the Jews, and it is still possible to study that law and discover some valuable lessons about salvation. The book of Hebrews helps us understand some of those lessons. The difference is that in the Old Testament the ceremonial law was one of the best ways the people had of learning about salvation, while for us today it is a very limited way. We have the story of Jesus in the four Gospels, and Paul and the other New Testament writers gave us a grand expansion on the meaning of Christ's life and death. So while we can say that one proper function of law in the New Testament is to teach us about the plan of salvation, we must also understand the severe limitations of this function of law since the cross. We must not depend on the Old Testament sanctuary service as our primary source of understanding about grace and righteousness by faith.

In the Old Testament the law also provided a way for God's people to enter into the experience of salvation. Is that function of law still in operation today? Of course not. That was Paul's whole point in his letter to the Galatians. It was the whole point of his conflict with the Jewish party. The Jewish party insisted that Christians in New Testament times had to enter into the experience of salvation the same way Jews did in Old Testament times, and Paul said, "No, that is an improper function of law." "No one," he said, "will be declared righteous in his sight [enter into the experience of salvation] by observing the law; rather, through the law we become conscious of sin" (Rom. 3:20).[2]

Paul stated right there the proper and improper functions of law in

New Testament times. We can actually divide this improper function of law into two parts. First, we cannot be saved by our efforts at keeping the moral law, and second, we cannot use the Old Testament ceremonial law as an entry point into the experience of salvation. We cannot use it to enter into a faith relationship with Jesus Christ and God. This was a proper function of law in Old Testament times. God ordained it that way. But it is an improper function of law today.

Now let's diagram the proper and improper functions of law in the New Testament era:

NEW TESTAMENT	
Proper function of law	**Improper function of law**
1. As a way to learn about sin 2. As a limited way to learn grace and God's plan of salvation	1. As a way to gain favor with God 2. As a symbolic way to enter into the experience of salvation

This point about the proper and improper function of law is important as we go into Galatians 3:23-25 and try to understand what Paul meant when he talked about the schoolmaster.

So far in this chapter we have discussed only the first two sentences of Galatians 3:19—Paul's question, "What, then, was the purpose of the law?" and his answer, "It was added because of transgressions until the Seed to whom the promise referred had come." Furthermore, we have discussed only briefly his crucial words "Until the Seed . . . had come." This phrase needs much more attention than we have given it in this chapter, but we will do that in the next chapter.

Before leaving the present chapter, though, we need to consider briefly Paul's words in the last half of Galatians 3:19 and all of verse 20. Paul said, "The law was put into effect through angels by a mediator. A mediator, however, does not represent just one party; but God is one."

At first glance these words appear to have no relationship whatso-ever to Paul's line of reasoning up to this point. What has the fact that the law was given through angels by a mediator have to do with the perpetuity of the promise, even after the giving of the law? And what has the fact that a mediator represents more than one party, but God is one, have to do with this argument?

Early in this book I pointed out that Paul's meaning in Galatians is often less than transparent to us because he assumed that the members of the Galatian church were completely familiar with the arguments of the Jewish party, whereas we have to infer their arguments from what Paul said. This passage probably caused the Galatian Christians no problem whatsoever. Unfortunately, there is little to nothing either in the context or elsewhere in the Bible that helps us understand Paul's meaning. However, one bit of information from scholarly research into the Jewish literature of Paul's time may help.

It was commonly believed by both Christians and Jews at Paul's time that God transmitted the law at Sinai to Moses through angels, who gave it to the Israelites. (In three places the Bible suggests that angels had a part to play in the giving of the law at Sinai [see Acts 7:53; Heb. 2:2; and Deut. 33:2, especially the Greek Septuagint].) This appears to be the best explanation of Paul's statement that "the law was put into effect through angels by a mediator." The mediator, of course, would have been Moses. In other words, God gave the law to angels, who gave it to Moses, who gave it to the people. We find a similar statement in Revelation 1:1, 2, which says that God gave the Apocalypse to Jesus, who gave it to an angel, who gave it to John, who gave it to the churches.

But why would Paul bring this bit of tradition into his line of reasoning?

Keep in mind that Paul's main point thus far in this passage (Gal. 3:15-19) has been the superiority of the promise over the law. By his statement that the law was given through angels by the hand of a mediator, he apparently meant that the promise was superior because it was given to Abraham directly by God, whereas the law was transmitted indirectly through intermediaries. Coming to the people from angels by the hand of a mediator, it would have been twice removed from a direct communication from God Himself. This further substantiates the conclusion that by "law" in Galatians Paul had much more in mind than the Ten Commandments, since the Ten Commandments *were* spoken directly to the people by God.

Going on to verse 20, what did Paul mean when he said that "a mediator . . . does not represent just one party; but God is one"? Paul's meaning here has so far escaped readers since the first century that to date it has received more than 250 explanations! One commentator went so far as to say that "of verse 20 it has been said there are as many interpretations as the number of years [430] between promise and law!" (Fung, *Galatians*, p. 161; see also *The SDA Bible Commentary*, vol. 6, p. 960).

According to one of these 250 (or 430) explanations, an agreement between two or more parties is weaker than a fiat that can be handed down unilaterally by a single person who has great authority. One party to a contract between two or more people may break the contract, but nobody can overturn what has been enforced by a single individual who has great authority. Thus, the law, which was an agreement between God and the Israelites, and which was transmitted through angels by a mediator, was of less significance than the promise, which was given to Abraham directly by God, who is just one person with supreme authority.

No one can be sure what Paul meant in Galatians 3:20, but this explanation appeals to me because it harmonizes with the whole thrust of his argument up to this point in the Epistle.

This concludes our discussion of Galatians 3:19, 20. The background we have discovered here will be crucial as we study verses 21-25.

---

[1] Obviously no Jew could bring a lamb to the sanctuary and later to the Temple for every sin committed. In the first place, most Jews would have lived far enough from Jerusalem to make frequent trips there impossible. And unless the Jews were holier than the average Christian today, even the best of them would soon have gone bankrupt. The law, however, provided for this also in the morning and evening sacrifices, which were offered on behalf of the entire nation.

[2] I am admittedly making a specific application of this text in Romans. The Jews in the Old Testament were not saved by works any more than Christians have been.

The Gospel According to Sinai—Part 2
Galatians 3:21-24

O n October 17, 1888, 91 delegates gathered in a newly constructed Adventist church in Minneapolis, Minnesota, to attend the twenty-seventh session of the General Conference of Seventh-day Adventists. That General Conference session has gone down in Adventist history as a turning point in our understanding of righteousness by faith. Several years ago, when we celebrated the Minneapolis session's one hundredth anniversary, the major emphasis in Adventist books and journals was on the 1888 conference and its contribution to the doctrine of righteousness by faith.

Interestingly enough, though, the delegates themselves had no such thoughts in their heads. Imagine, for instance, that you were a delegate traveling to Minneapolis on October 16, 1888, that you died in a train wreck on the way, and that you were resurrected 100 years later to help celebrate the one-hundredth anniversary. You would certainly be very surprised to discover that the 1888 General Conference session had anything at all to do with righteousness by faith. The subject was not even on the agenda! Even if you had attended the session, died in a train wreck on the way home, and come to life 100 years later, you would almost certainly be surprised that 1888 was a landmark event in the Adventist understanding of righteousness by faith.

Two items were announced in advance for discussion at the conference. One was the 10 horns of Daniel 7, and the other was the law in Galatians. The weighty issue regarding the 10 horns was whether the tenth horn represented the Huns or the Alemanni. Uriah Smith, the acknowledged Adventist authority on prophetic interpretation for 40 years, held out for the Huns, while young A. T. Jones argued for the Alemanni. The delegates at Minneapolis exhausted an incredible amount of emotional energy, and not a few heated words, over an issue that to us seems superficial in the extreme. We shake our heads and smile.

The question of the law in Galatians is admittedly far more significant.

PAGE
93

The primary issue was whether Paul's "schoolmaster" analogy in Galatians 3:24, 25 referred to the moral or the ceremonial law. The lines were drawn between tradition and "new theology." Uriah Smith and General Conference president George I. Butler defended the traditional view that the schoolmaster referred to the ceremonial law.[1] On the other side were A. T. Jones and E. J. Waggoner, two young men from California who were coeditors of the *Signs of the Times* and professors at Pacific Union College. Waggoner made the actual presentations on Galatians, in which he insisted that the schoolmaster was the moral law.

However, Waggoner's major emphasis was not on the law in Galatians. He conducted at least 11 meetings on Galatians over a period of several days, and his main focus of attention was on what Galatians says about justification by faith. Thus, the subject of justification (or righteousness) by faith *was* a point of lively discussion at the session; it just was not the *announced* point of discussion. To their credit, Adventists since that time have remembered 1888 far more for what was said about righteousness by faith than for what was said about the law in Galatians.

As we approach the study of Galatians 3, it would be well for us to keep Waggoner's perspective. We will fail of truly understanding Paul's theology of law in Galatians if we separate it from his theology of the gospel and righteousness by faith. For Paul, the issues were spiritual. They were theological only because theology affects spirituality. It is imperative that we approach our study of Galatians 3:21-25 the same way. Let's begin our study by quoting these verses: "Is the law, therefore, opposed to the promises of God? Absolutely not! For if a law had been given that could impart life, then righteousness would certainly have come by the law. But the Scripture declares that the whole world is a prisoner of sin, so that what was promised, being given through faith in Jesus Christ, might be given to those who believe. Before this faith came, we were held prisoners by the law, locked up until faith should be revealed. So the law was put in charge to lead us to Christ that we might be justified by faith. Now that faith has come, we are no longer under the supervision of the law."

The problem sentence here is the last one: "Now that faith has come, we are no longer under the supervision of the law." This is the New International Version's translation of the "schoolmaster" verse in the King James Version. Perhaps we ought to read verses 23-25 from the King James: "But before faith came, we were kept under the law, shut up unto the faith which should afterwards be revealed. Wherefore the law was our schoolmaster *to bring us* unto Christ, that we might be justified by faith. But after that faith is come, we are no longer under a schoolmaster."

I think you can see the problem this passage poses for Seventh-day Adventists. It's unthinkable to us that God's people should no longer be under the moral law. This statement in Galatians 3:24 presents the same problem as verse 19, where Paul said that the law was introduced "because of transgressions *until the Seed . . . had come."*

Our earliest Adventist pioneers adopted the view that the schoolmaster was the ceremonial law. There's a lot of truth to that, but Paul's argument goes much deeper than this, as we will see. Let's analyze verses 21 to 25, beginning with verse 21: "Is the law, therefore, opposed to the promises of God? Absolutely not! For if a law had been given that could impart life, then righteousness would certainly have come by the law."

In verses 15-18 Paul had argued that God made a legal contract with Abraham, promising him righteousness by faith, and the law, which was given on Sinai 430 years later, did not invalidate this promise. In verse 19 he raised the next obvious question: If the law didn't invalidate the promise, what was its function? And the answer: The law was added "because of transgressions" until Jesus should come. However, the answer to one question apparently raised another one in Paul's mind—or perhaps in the minds of his Jewish opponents: "Is the law *opposed* to the promise?" Are the law and the promise fighting each other?

Absolutely not, Paul said, because the law cannot impart life. His point is that the law has its function and the promise has its function, and these two are not in conflict with each other. To the contrary, they complement each other. The law points out sin and the promise gives life. The law exposes the sin that destroys us, and the promise exposes the Saviour who delivers us. If law could impart life, eternal life would be possible through keeping the law. But it would be impossible to devise a law that could give life.

Think of that for a moment. There are some things God cannot do, and one of them is this: He cannot make a law that people can obey and live forever. Had that been possible, God would surely have chosen that way to save sinners rather than giving up His Son to die for sin. But God *could not* make a law that would give life. If there is no way that a law could provide eternal life, then the only way to obtain it is through promise—through faith. That's why Paul said that the law and the promise are not in conflict with each other.

Now let's read verse 22: "But the Scripture declares that the whole world is a prisoner of sin, so that what was promised, being given through faith in Jesus Christ, might be given to those who believe."

Romans 3:10-18 helps us understand Paul's first sentence in verse 22, where he said, "The Scripture declares that the whole world is *a prisoner of sin.*" In Romans Paul said, "As it is written: 'There is no one righteous, not even one; there is no one who understands, no one who seeks God. All have turned away, they have together become worthless; there is no one who does good, not even one.' 'Their throats are open graves; their tongues practice deceit.' 'The poison of vipers is on their lips.' 'Their mouths are full of cursing and bitterness.' 'Their feet are swift to shed blood; ruin and misery mark their ways, and the way of peace they do not know.' 'There is no fear of God before their eyes.'"

What a terrible picture! Yet Paul was talking about the same thing in Galatians: "The whole world is a prisoner of sin."

Why did Paul say that the whole world is a prisoner of sin? The average non-Christian thinks of this as pure condemnation, as though God were up in heaven with a big whip in His hand, trying to figure out how many people He can beat into line. But I would like to suggest that anytime God speaks harshly about sin, He's trying to get our attention. He's trying to help us understand that our hearts are infected with a deadly disease. We call this divine activity "conviction." So when God condemns the world for being sinful, He's actually appealing to us to give up our sins so we can have eternal life. One of the most beautiful pictures of God's conviction of sin anywhere in the Bible is found in the story of the prodigal son, who said, "Father, I have sinned against heaven and against you. I am no longer worthy to be called your son; make me like one of your hired men" (Luke 15:18, 19).

When God declares that the whole world is a prisoner of sin, like the prodigal son's father, He's looking for a reason to celebrate. He's hoping that a few people at least will recognize their sinfulness and repent. There's more joy in heaven over one sinner who repents than over 99 who need no repentance. Salvation is the primary reason why God declares everyone a sinner. And that's exactly the reason Paul gave in Galatians 3:22: "The scripture declares that the whole world is a prisoner of sin, *so that what was promised [eternal life], being given through faith in Jesus Christ, might be given to those who believe.*"

Let's get a bit technical about verse 22. There are two or three points we need to notice. First is the word "Scripture." Paul said, "Scripture declares that the whole world is a prisoner of sin." This is similar to what he said in Romans 3:20: "Through the law we become conscious of sin." Notice also that Paul concluded Galatians 3:21 with the word "law": "Then righteousness would certainly have come by the law." If he said that law convicts of sin in Romans 3:20, and if he concluded Galatians 3:21 with the word "law," then why didn't he say, in Galatians 3:22, "The *law* declares that the whole world is a prisoner of sin"?

Commentators have puzzled over this apparent oddity almost since Paul wrote his letter to the Galatians, and I don't know that anyone has come up with the right answer. We will have to wait for the answer until we can ask Paul himself in heaven. However, I will suggest a couple of possibilities.

The simplest answer may be that we shouldn't attach any theological significance to Paul's use of the word "Scripture." It may be that as he dictated his letter (see Gal. 6:11), he inadvertently used the word "Scripture" here instead of "law," and by the time he noticed the inconsistency it was too late to change it. Paul did not, after all, live in our day and age when correcting a writing error is a matter of a few keystrokes on the computer and running out a new page on the laser printer. To correct his mistake he would at the very least have had to make a messy scratch through the wrong word and insert a new one, or, worse still, throw away the whole expensive parchment on which his scribe was writing and start over with a new one. It may be that after he noticed his slip of the tongue he said something like "I wish I'd said law there instead of Scripture, but Scripture is correct enough. Let's leave well enough alone."

On the other hand, we must consider the possibility that Paul made a conscious choice to say Scripture instead of law. If so, what was his reason? My own best guess is that he wanted to avoid confusing his meaning in verse 22 with his meaning in verse 23. This is a fine point that we do not need to discuss in detail here, lest we interrupt our investigation of Paul's main point overly much.

Paul said, "Scripture declares that the whole world *is* a prisoner of sin." Notice that I italicized the word *is*. I did that to call attention to the fact that it is in the present tense. The significance of this lies in the fact that just about everything else in verses 19 to 25 is in the past tense. For example, in verse 21 Paul said, "If a law *had been given* that could impart life, then righteousness would certainly *have come* by the law," and in verse 23 he said, "Before this faith came, we *were* held prisoners by the law." The reason nearly everything else in verses 19 to 25 is in the past tense is that Paul's primary purpose throughout this passage was to explain the role of law during the Jewish era of Old Testament history. But if you'll look carefully, that was not his purpose in verse 22. Here he said, "The Scripture declares that the *whole world* is a prisoner of sin"—the whole world, not just the Jewish nation. That's why he said that "the whole world *is* a prisoner of sin"—present tense.

Keep in mind that Paul wrote these words some 25 to 30 years after the cross. So when he said that "the whole world *is* a prisoner of sin," he was making a statement about his own time. This is a universal statement about the sinful condition of human beings in every age, not just the Jews between Sinai and Calvary. This point will be significant in our discussion of verse 23.

The first thing we need to notice as we get into verse 23 is that Paul began saying "we" again and kept up this "we" point of view for the next several verses. We found this same point of view back in Galatians 2:15, where Paul said, "We who are Jews by birth and not Gentile sinners." In chapter 2 he wanted his readers to know that he was talking specifically to Jews about Jews and not to Gentiles about Gentiles. Paul had the same reason in mind when he resumed this "we" point of view in Galatians 3:23. He wanted to explain to the Galatian Christians the purpose of the law for the Jews before Jesus came.

Paul began verse 23 by saying, "Before this faith came." What faith did he have in mind? And before what, or before whom? The answer is found in the previous verse, where Paul said that the Bible has declared the whole world to be a prisoner of sin, "so that what was promised, being given through *faith* in Jesus Christ, might be given to those who believe." Clearly, then, when Paul said "Before this faith came," he meant before Christ's time.

And what happened before Christ's time? "Before this faith came, *we were held prisoners by the law, locked up until faith should be revealed.*"

Some Bible commentators have concluded that Paul meant righteousness by faith was available after Christ. However, such a conclusion misses the whole point of Paul's argument thus far in Galatians. If that's what he had meant, he would have *joined* the Jewish party, not *opposed* them. *They* were the ones insisting that the law superseded the promise to Abraham. Paul said no. Righteousness by faith began with Abraham and continued uninterrupted until Christ's time.

This is not to say that everything about the relationship of the Jews to the law before the cross was identical to the relationship Christians have to the law after the cross. There *was* a difference. Paul did not deny that. To the contrary, he affirmed it. If there had been no difference between the function of law in the lives of God's people before the cross than there was after the cross, Paul presumably would not have had a conflict with the Jewish party. They were the ones insisting that there was no difference. Paul wrote Galatians to show that there was a difference and to explain what that difference was. Some Christians think that when Paul spoke of the law functioning until Christ came he meant that it was done away with after Christ. But Paul was not doing away with the law after Christ. He was telling us that the law functioned differently before Christ from the way it functioned after Christ.

We are now entering the final phase of our effort to understand what Paul meant when he said that after Christ came, "we are no longer under a schoolmaster." To do that, we need to consider verses 23 and 24 together. Apparently Paul was particularly anxious for his readers to understand his point in these verses, because he used three Greek words to explain it. I will quote verses 23 and 24 below, with the English translation of these words italicized: "Before this faith came, we were *held prisoners* by the law, *locked up* until faith should be revealed. So the law was *put in charge* to lead us to Christ, that we might be justified by faith."

Below is a chart that shows the three Greek words we will be examining, together with the way they have been translated by the King James Version and the New International Version:

GREEK	KJV	NIV
Phroureō	"kept under"	"help prisoners"
Sygkleiō	"shut up"	"locked up"
Paidagōgos	"schoolmaster"	"put in charge"

Let's analyze these words, starting with *phroureō*. You will notice that the King James Version translates this word "kept under," whereas the New International Version says "held prisoners." In my library I have a Greek lexicon by Arndt and Gingrich—one of the most widely accepted dictionaries of biblical Greek in existence today. According to Arndt and Gingrich, *phroureō* means "to guard," "to hold in custody," "to confine," but they do not say that *phroureō* means "to imprison." Obviously prisoners are guarded, held in custody, and confined, so the NIV is not incorrect in taking *phroureō* to mean "held prisoner."[2] But we can also guard things, hold them in custody, and confine them without locking them up in prison. Prison is a terribly severe way of confining a person. It implies some wrongdoing on the part of the person so confined. It is my personal conviction that Paul did not intend to describe the function of law for Jews before Christ in such harsh terms. However, we need to examine all three of these Greek words before trying to decide Paul's meaning in any one of them.

Let's look at the second word that Paul used in Galatians 3:23—*sygkleiō*, which the King James Version translates "shut up" and the NIV translates "locked up." Arndt and Gingrich's lexicon does mention imprison as one possible translation of *sygkleiō*. However, it also says that it can mean "to confine" or "to enclose." So which are we to understand—the more harsh idea of putting in prison or the more gentle idea of confining or enclosing? The context has to help us determine the best English translation. As we have already seen, in Galatians 3:19-25 Paul was trying to explain the proper function of law for Jews between Sinai and Calvary. We have also seen that he held a high regard for law before the cross. It was a great advantage over the patriarchal system that had existed before Sinai. Because of this, I think "imprison" is too negative an English term to use in explaining the function of law between Sinai and Calvary.

The validity of this conclusion becomes even clearer when we examine the third word that Paul used to explain the function of law during the Jewish period of Old Testament history: *paidagōgos*. This is the word that is translated "schoolmaster" in the King James Version. The *paidagōgos* in Roman society was "a guardian of children," "a companion to boys. He accompanied them to school, protected them from harm, kept them from mischief, and had the right to discipline them. In Greek art he is generally represented as having a stick in his hand" (*The SDA Bible Commentary,* vol. 6, p. 961). Think for a moment of the picture we get from *paidagōgos*

—a guardian of children who is to protect them from harm, keep them out of mischief, and discipline them when they disobey. This hardly conveys the idea of harsh, cold imprisonment!

One other factor leads me to the conclusion that Paul did not have the severe idea of prison in mind when he wrote Galatians 3:23, 24. In 1 Peter 1:5 we find another occurrence of the word *phroureō,* and in some respects it is used there in the same way that Paul used it in Galatians: "Praise be to the God and Father of our Lord Jesus Christ! In his great mercy he has given us new birth into a living hope through the resurrection of Jesus Christ from the dead, and into an inheritance that can never perish, spoil or fade—kept in heaven for you, who through faith are shielded [*phroureō*] by God's power until the coming of the salvation that is ready to be revealed in the last time" (1 Peter 1:3-5).

Let's put the way the NIV translates *phroureō* in Galatians side by side with the way it translates the same word in 1 Peter so we can compare them:

Galatians 3:23	1 Peter 1:5
Before this faith came, we were *held prisoners* by the law . . . until faith should be revealed.	**You, who through faith are *shielded* by God's power until the coming of the salvation that is ready to be revealed.**

The italicized words in each of these paragraphs come from *phroureō.* Notice that the NIV translates the word "held prisoners" in Galatians, while in 1 Peter it says "shielded." There is a certain similarity between holding a person prisoner and shielding him. We might say that a prisoner is shielded from the outside world. However, shielded carries more the idea of protection than it does of confinement in a prison. As we examine Paul's use of this word in Galatians 3:23, we must remember that God had a beneficial purpose in mind when He gave the law at Sinai. Restricting as it may seem to us, it was liberating in its time. Thus, "shielded" comes much closer to expressing God's purpose in giving the law than does "held prisoner."

If this is true, why does the NIV translate *phroureō* to mean "held prisoner" (as do *The New English Bible* and Today's English Version)? First, we must remember that the word can properly be translated "held prisoner." Second, the translators may have understood *phroureō* to mean "held prisoner" because they were thinking of Paul's harsh language against law in other places. They failed to recognize that in this instance Paul was trying to explain the right use of law in the Old Testament, not its misuse by the Jewish party in the New Testament.

So let's try substituting the word "shielded" for "held prisoner" in Galatians 3:23 and see how that sounds: "Before this faith came, we were *shielded* by the law." Can you tell the difference? The word "shielded" conveys much more the beneficial purpose for which God gave the law to His people at Sinai. To really get the point, let's do the switch the other way. Let's transfer the NIV's "held prisoner" in Galatians to 1 Peter: You "who through faith are *held prisoner* by God's power until the coming of the salvation that is ready to be revealed." That doesn't sound quite right, does it? I'd like to suggest that it is no more right in Galatians than it is in 1 Peter.

This conclusion is borne out even more strongly when we notice one other similarity between Galatians 3:23 and 1 Peter 1:5. In Galatians Paul said that the Jews were shielded by the law *until the first coming of Jesus,* and Peter said God's people in the New Testament era are shielded by God's power *until the second coming of Jesus.*[2] The law in the Old Testament and God's power in the New Testament—in each case God provided a shield to hold His people in protective custody until the next great event in salvation history.

It is my personal conviction that Paul thought of the law as a protector of God's Old Testament people—as a fence around them to keep them from going astray, as a guardian to convict them *of* sin and help them understand His plan to save them *from* sin. Furthermore, I believe Paul had in mind not only the law as such but also the Jewish religion that developed out of the law. Genuine Judaism protected God's people just as the church and the Christian faith protect us today.

We might compare it to a mother confining her baby in a playpen until it is old enough to be outside without getting into trouble. The playpen is confining, yet it is also a protection to the baby. The mother uses it, not because she is trying to be harsh or because she wants to remove the baby's freedom; she knows that her baby *needs* the protection of the playpen at this stage of its life. Similarly, during the Old Testament era, the Jewish religion and the law were a protection to God's people, a shield over them, a hedge about them—not because God wanted to imprison them, but because He knew they needed that protection until the full revelation of Jesus Christ came.

There are still two more phrases that we need to consider in Galatians 3:24, and then we will spend a bit of time with the most critical verse of them all—Galatians 3:25. I have quoted verses 23, 24 below. The two phrases we have yet to consider are italicized, and I have distinguished them with numbers. I will use the wording of the NIV, except that I will substitute "shielded" for "held prisoner," "confined" for "locked up," and "guardian" for "put in charge": "Before this faith came, we were shielded by the law, confined until faith should be revealed. So the law was our guardian [1] *to lead us to Christ* [2] *that we might be justified by faith*."

To lead us to Christ. The words "to lead us to" have been inserted. Most Bible translations, including the King James Version, add these words to the text, but they do not appear in the original language. The Greek says, "So the law was our guardian *until* Christ," not "*to lead us to* Christ." (The NIV margin says: "[put in] charge until Christ came.")

Why do most translators insert the words "to lead us to"? First, it's important to understand that there is nothing theologically wrong with adding these words to the text. Certainly by pointing out our sins the law shows us our need of a Saviour and thus leads us to Christ. Furthermore, it is in this very verse that Paul said the law was a *paidagōgos*—a guide, a guardian. If the *paidagōgos* led children to school, why shouldn't the law, as our *paidagōgos*, lead us to Christ? There are good reasons for inserting the words "to lead us to" here, making Paul say that "the law was our schoolmaster *to lead us to* Christ."

However, because the words "to lead us to" *are* inserted, we must ask whether they really belong there, and my personal conclusion is that they do not. I believe the passage ought to read in English just as it does in the Greek: "So the law was put in charge [was our guardian] until Christ." This wording fits the context better. Twice before, in Galatians 3:19-24, Paul said that the law served a particular function *until Christ came*; why not here? Let's put these other two occurrences together with the one in verse 24 and look at all of them together. I have italicized the relevant words: Verse 19: "[The law] was added . . . *until the Seed . . . had come.*" Verse 23: "*Before this faith came*, we were held prisoners by the law" (the implication is that after the faith came we were no longer held prisoners by the law). Verse 24: "So the law was put in charge *until Christ.*"

Since Paul's purpose in Galatians 3:19-25 was to explain the function of law in the lives of God's people between Sinai and Calvary, why shouldn't we let him say that in verse 24? Why should we obscure his meaning by inserting "to lead us to"? Although there is nothing theologically wrong with saying that the law was our guardian to lead us to Christ, we misunderstand what Paul really meant when we add these words.

"That we might be justified by faith" (verse 24). This is an extremely important phrase. It is the high point of Paul's argument so far in Galatians. Everything else falls into place when we understand what Paul meant here.

At the risk of being horribly redundant, let's review Paul's argument in the past 10 verses one more time. God gave Abraham the promise of righteousness by faith, and He "signed a contract" with him that could not be broken. Thus, it was impossible that the law, which came 430 years later, should annul the promise. To the contrary, the promise continued in effect side by side with the law. Obviously, according to this line of reasoning, the Jews were saved by faith between Sinai and Calvary. To say otherwise would be to say that the law in fact *did* do away with the promise.

And that's the whole point of the phrase we are considering: "The law was put in charge until Christ *that we might be justified by faith."*

In other words, the law actually *helped* God's Old Testament people be saved by faith. The law was instituted *in order that* they might be justified by faith while they awaited the One who was the object of their faith. Justification by faith would have been harder during Old Testament times without the law. It was made easier with the law.

There are at least two reasons this is true. First, as we have already noted, the moral law pointed out sin, making it easier for the people to recognize their need of a Saviour and prompting them to come to Him for help (the law *did* lead to Christ, even though that's not what Paul actually said in this instance). The second reason why law made it easier for Jews in the Old Testament to be justified by faith is that the ceremonial law was actually the gospel stated in terms of law, giving them a ritual they could go through to introduce them to the gospel.

A few modern Bible translators have suggested a slightly different meaning to this phrase in verse 24. Notice how three of them have worded it:

The New English Bible: "Thus the law was a kind of tutor in
charge of us until Christ should come, when we should be
justified through faith."

The Living Bible: "The Jewish laws were our teacher and guide
until Christ came to give us right standing with God [justifi-
cation] through our faith."

Today's English Version: "And so the Law was in charge of us
until Christ came, in order that we might then be put right
with God through faith."

Read these three translations of verse 24 carefully, and you will see
that each one seems to suggest that in some way justification by faith became available only when Christ came. However, I don't think that's what
Paul meant here. Paul insisted throughout this part of Galatians that justification by faith was given to Abraham, and it continued to be God's way of
saving people throughout the Old Testament period. If these translators
were trying to make Paul say that justification by faith was not available at
all until Christ came, then they missed the whole point of Paul's argument
thus far in his letter to the Galatians.

It is possible that the translators understood justification by faith in Old
Testament times to be a promise that had not yet been made legal by
Christ's death on the cross. Thus, while God's people in Old Testament
times were indeed justified by faith, they looked forward to Christ, who
would validate their faith by His death. Although this view is correct
enough in itself, I don't think that's what Paul had in mind in this passage.

We have finally come to Galatians 3:25. The question is What did Paul
mean when he said, "Now that faith has come, we are no longer under the
supervision of the law"? Or, as the King James Version says it, "But after that
faith is come, we are no longer under a schoolmaster." The schoolmaster is,
of course, the law. Paul appears to mean that Christians after the cross are
no longer under the law. However, in Romans Paul makes it utterly clear
that law continues to have a proper place in the life of Christians. He says,
"Through the law we become conscious of sin" (Rom. 3:20). "I would not
have known what sin was except through the law" (7:7). And "the law is
holy, and the commandment is holy, righteous and good" (7:12).

All the theology we have discussed up to this point provides the background for our understanding of Galatians 3:25 and its apparent contradiction of Paul's teaching about law in Romans. The solution to this problem

is so important that I have devoted an entire chapter to an interpretation of this one verse. Let's turn to it now.

---

[1] Because of an illness Butler was not able to attend the session, but his influence was pervasive just the same.

[2] The English preposition *until* in Galatians 3:23 comes from the Greek preposition *eis*, the primary meaning of which is "into." However, prepositions in all languages are used to express a variety of meanings. One of the secondary meanings of *eis* is "until," which is clearly the meaning to be preferred in this instance.

The word *eis* is not the Greek word behind "until" in 1 Peter 1:5. My comparison of Galatians 3:23 with 1 Peter 1:5 is based on the NIV translation. It would be ideal for the point I am making had Peter used the same preposition that Paul used. However, I believe my comparison is faithful to Peter's meaning as it is suggested by the context, and the NIV translators clearly agree.

CHAPTER 12

No Longer Under a Schoolmaster
Galatians 3:25

We have now come to the verse that caused such an uproar at the 1888 General Conference session in Minneapolis. This is the verse that, at first glance, appears to state so unequivocally that the law was done away with when Christ came. Such an interpretation is naturally a great threat to our Adventist emphasis on the importance of law in the life of the Christian. Our pioneers, in an effort to counter that threat, interpreted the schoolmaster to mean the ceremonial law. And in a real sense this is true. As we have seen, the ceremonial law was an important part of what Paul meant by the schoolmaster. However, we have also seen that much more was included. To limit the schoolmaster to the ceremonial law is to apply a "quick fix" to the problem. Unfortunately, our quick fixes tend to become permanent fixes, locked into doctrine. Those who come later with a more studied solution to the problem are then perceived as a threat to "the truth," which is, in reality, simply a surface solution to the problem. That, in essence, is the dynamic that was operating at the 1888 General Conference session in Minneapolis.

Yet interestingly enough, Jones and Waggoner (and Waggoner in particular, since he made the presentations on Galatians) also applied a "quick fix" to the problem. From my reading of the writings of these two men, it appears to me that while they came closer to the truth than Smith and Butler, they were still wide of the mark. They still did not understand the "caretaker" function of the law that we discussed in the previous chapter. They failed to understand that in verses 23 and 24 Paul was defining the unique role of law for Jews between Sinai and Calvary. They thought the "we" pronouns in verses 23-25 referred to God's people in any age, including Christians since the cross. Since they believed, correctly, that the schoolmaster includes the moral law—and since they believed, again correctly, that the moral law still points out sin—they had to believe that Christians are still under a schoolmaster. And they said so.

But Paul said that "we are no longer under a schoolmaster." Jones and

Waggoner's quick fix actually contradicted a plain statement of Scripture! Their view was theologically correct, and it was about the only conclusion they could have drawn, given their view that the "we" pronouns in Galatians 3:23-25 include Christians since the cross. Jones and Waggoner allowed their theology to influence their interpretation of Scripture when they should have let Scripture influence their theology. If Scripture said that "we are no longer under a schoolmaster," they should have tried to understand how that was true instead of bending Scripture or denying a plain statement of Scripture in order to accommodate their theology.

Our effort in this book, and especially in the previous few chapters, has been to get behind the quick fixes, the traditions, and the theological presuppositions on both sides and try to understand what Paul really meant by law and schoolmaster in Galatians 3.

We have now come to Galatians 3:25. This verse is the capstone of Paul's response to the Jewish party's view of law. The Jewish party's view was being widely accepted by the churches in Galatia, and Paul recognized it as a severe threat to the gospel that Jesus had revealed to him. He wrote his letter to the Galatians to counter that threat. Up to this point in the epistle he has taken great pains to clarify the function of law in the Old Testament between Sinai and Calvary, and to explain the relationship of this function of law to the promise of righteousness by faith that God gave to Abraham. Verse 25 is his summary statement.

"Now that faith has come," he said, "we are no longer under the supervision of the law." The King James Version says, "After that faith is come, we are no longer under a schoolmaster."

Let's analyze this short verse, beginning with the first clause, "Now that faith has come."

It would be a serious mistake to think that Paul meant faith was unavailable as a way of salvation before the cross. His whole argument up to this point has been that the law given on Sinai did not annul the promise of righteousness by faith given 430 years earlier to Abraham. Galatians 3:25 cannot be made to contradict everything Paul said in the previous 10 or 12 verses. Whatever he meant by the word "faith" in verse 25, he did not intend us to understand that faith as a means for gaining salvation began only at the cross—not when in the previous verse he emphasized that the law was given at Sinai in order "that we [God's people between Sinai and the cross] might be justified by *faith*." Paul's use of faith in verse

25 *has* to be different from his use of the word in verse 24, or he would contradict himself. But what is the difference?

I believe that in verse 25 Paul means faith as a system, in contrast to law as a system. He means much the same as when we say "Keep the faith," or when we speak of "the Christian faith," "the Baptist faith," or "the Adventist faith." Faith in this sense is a belief system. Christianity grew out of the belief system that began at the cross, just as Judaism grew out of the belief system that began at Sinai. So in a real sense we can say that as a final summation of his explanation of the unique function of law for Jews before Christ, Paul contrasted the two religions that grew out of the two belief systems. He said, in essence, that Christianity replaced Judaism as a guardian to carry God's people toward the final end of all things.

Now that we understand what Paul meant by "faith" in the first half of verse 25, we need to ask what he meant in the last half when he said that "we are no longer under the supervision of the law."

Of one thing we can be sure: he did *not* mean that law ceased to have any valid function after the cross. That much is clear from his own statement in verse 22, where he said, "The Scripture [the law] declares that the whole world is a prisoner of sin." Several passages in Romans make it clear that the law continues to point out sin in the New Testament era (see Rom. 3:19; 5:20; 7:7, 13).

When Paul said that we are no longer under the supervision of the law (schoolmaster), he meant that the function of law as a guardian, as a hedge about God's people, was over with. It was no longer an entry point to salvation. Christians do not have to approach God through human mediators with animal sacrifices to obtain forgiveness for our sins. We can approach Him directly through Jesus Christ. We no longer have the limited understanding of moral truth provided by words inscribed on stone. We now have the full revelation of moral principles in the words and in the life of God Himself, in the person of Jesus Christ. We are no longer shielded by law until the first coming of Christ. We are shielded by the power of God until the second coming of Christ. We are no longer under a schoolmaster. We are under the Headmaster!

At no time in the history of our world has God left His people without a way to approach Him for salvation. The first gospel (good news) was announced in Eden by God Himself when He said, "I will put enmity between you and the woman" (Gen. 3:15). We might call this "the gospel according to Eden." This gospel continued through the patriarchal period until God Himself announced an update at Sinai—what we have called "the gospel according to Sinai." This gospel—both the moral and the ceremonial law—continued for 1,500 years until again God Himself, in the person of Jesus Christ, announced yet another update. We might call this "the gospel according to Jesus Christ," or "the gospel according to Calvary." This gospel is to continue in effect until Jesus returns in power and glory at His second coming.

This gospel, the one you and I live under, includes both faith and law. Actually, there has never been a gospel that did not include both faith and law. The difference is that the gospel according to Sinai was organized around law, with faith as an important component, whereas the gospel according to Calvary is organized around faith, with law as an important component.

I would like to summarize in one short sentence—just three words— what I believe Paul meant in Galatians 3:25: Christianity replaced Judaism. Or, to use Paul's own language: "Now that Christianity has come, we are no longer under Judaism."

This was Paul's message to the Galatian Christians. This was his response to the Jewish party. And in this light we can perhaps understand why the Jewish party opposed him so fiercely. Jones and Waggoner confronted 40 years of a traditional interpretation that was in reality only a half truth, a "quick fix," and not the whole truth. Paul, on the other hand, faced 1,500 years of tradition that had developed around a gospel that had been given on Sinai by God Himself. The gospel according to Sinai was not a quick fix. It was God's truth, God's plan for His people for a millennium and a half. You don't do away with that kind of tradition with a snap of the fingers. If Butler and Smith had a hard time in Minneapolis with the views of two young upstarts from California, can we really blame the Jewish party for having a hard time with Paul?

I would now like to turn our attention to a practical question: What lesson is there in Galatians 3:10-25 for us? Much of our discussion in the past few chapters has been theoretical. That is unavoidable. There is really no other way to unravel a difficult passage such as Galatians 3:19-25, but once the theory is done, we need to ask what spiritual value there is behind the theory. This is a particularly important question for us, since we do not have a Jewish party hounding us about circumcision and the observance of Jewish feast days. In one sense this whole argument in Galatians is somewhat foreign to us. It's an interesting study of an ancient problem that on the surface appears to have little relationship to the problems we face today.

However, if we look beneath the surface, we will find many lessons that have a profound meaning for our own lives.

First is the fact that for us, the promise of a Redeemer is no longer a matter of faith. What a privilege is ours to have four Gospels that tell us about the life and ministry of Jesus Christ! We ought to cherish these stories, especially the story of the cross and the Resurrection. We have the story of the Holy Spirit's work in the New Testament church. We have the Epistles of Paul, Peter, James, and John to interpret the meaning of Jesus' life, death, and resurrection. We have the book of Revelation, given to John on Patmos, that guides us through the centuries of Christian history to the end of all things. Paul's basic message to the Galatians was a shout: "Look, people, at what God has done for you in Jesus Christ—and you're going to trade all that to remain under a limited system that is only a type of the real?"

We today are hardly under any great pressure to revert to Judaism. But have we nevertheless lost sight of the tremendous privilege that is ours to live under the gospel according to Calvary? Have we become so used to it as to be indifferent to it? Do we today need Paul's ringing words "Now that the faith has come"? And the answer is yes. Until Jesus comes, we must remember how fortunate we are to live after Calvary, not before; to know Jesus personally; to be able to approach His throne of grace directly rather than through a human mediator with an animal at our side.

Although we are not under any threat to revert to Judaism, Galatians 3 teaches us that we must never substitute any system of works for the gospel of righteousness by faith. Judaism in its day was an appropriate protector of God's people, a system that led them into the experience of righteousness by faith. The Jewish party's problem was that when God instituted a new system for leading His people into righteousness by faith, they insisted on perpetuating the old system. We are not in any danger of perpetuating the old Jewish system, but are we in danger of introducing a system of our own devising? And the answer, I believe, is yes. How easy it is to think that our adherence to dietary laws, rules for adornment, and standards for entertainment and Sabbathkeeping assures us of a place in God's kingdom. How easy it is to think that these form the basic system that leads us to Christ and the experience of righteousness by faith. How easy it is for us to think that those who obey the rules are the good people and those who violate them according to our perception are the bad people.

Another lesson that I learn from Galatians and the experience of our own church in Minneapolis is humility. How easy it is for us, like the Jewish party or those who opposed Jones and Waggoner at Minneapolis, to be so sure that our view is the only right view that we are intolerant of anyone else's views. How easy it is to rise to the defense of traditional truth only to be all wrong!

Galatians 3 means one final thing to me. As free as you and I are under the present system, and as fortunate as we are to live under that system and not the previous one, what a glorious privilege awaits us when we are delivered from this system and introduced to the next one! Surely, when we get to heaven, we will look back with relief on the system under which we now live—relief that in heaven we no longer have to live under it. We will thank God *then* that we have escaped from a system based on faith just as much as we thank Him *now* that we have escaped a system based on law. While a faith system for approaching God is far superior to a law system for approaching Him, it is still confining. We still cannot actually *see* Him. We hope for the New Jerusalem now, but someday we will actually walk its streets. How confining our present system of faith will seem to us then! No wonder Peter said that through faith we are "shielded by God's power until the coming salvation that is ready to be revealed"(1 Peter 1:5)!

CHAPTER 13

Sons and Daughters of God
Galatians 3:26-4:20

O n a Sunday afternoon in February 1992 I was flying home from a trip I had taken the week before for Pacific Press Publishing Association, where I work. Shortly after 3:00 the pilot's voice came on the plane's intercom system and told the flight attendants to prepare for landing. I knew what that meant, so I folded up the tray table in front of me and looked out the window. The winter landscape east of Boise seemed bleak. I watched as the ground got closer and closer. Soon I could tell that we were coming in for the landing.

As we approached the landing strip I happened to glance ahead, and I did a double take. To the left and a few hundred feet in front was a small plane flying backward. I couldn't believe it! Of course, a moment later I realized that the plane ahead wasn't flying backward at all. Each plane was approaching a different landing strip, and the Boeing 727 that I was on was actually overtaking the smaller aircraft quite rapidly, making it *seem* to fly backward. Reality wasn't what it appeared to be.

You'll want to keep this principle in mind as we get into the last few verses of Galatians 3 and the first half of chapter 4. Reality may not be what it appears to be when we first look at it.

As we begin the last part of chapter 3, we need to keep in mind Paul's line of reasoning. Up to this point in Galatians, and particularly in chapter 3, he has been explaining the relationship of the Jews to God *before* Calvary—a relationship that was based on law. However, in verse 26 he began to explain the relationship of both Jews and Gentiles to God *after* Calvary. We will seriously misunderstand Paul if we fail to recognize this shift. This is what can easily cause reality to be different from what it appears to be.

Also, beginning with verse 26 Paul introduced "sonship" into his argument against the Jewish party. This is a new concept that we have not found heretofore in Galatians. Let's read what Paul said in the last four verses of chapter 3: "You are all sons of God through faith in Christ Jesus, for all of you who were baptized into Christ have clothed yourselves with

Christ. There is neither Jew nor Greek, slave nor free, male nor female, for you are all one in Christ Jesus. If you belong to Christ, then you are Abraham's seed, and heirs according to the promise" (verses 26-29).

Sonship is a familiar New Testament concept. John wrote, "But as many as received him, to them gave he power to become the sons of God" (John 1:12, KJV). And in his first letter the same apostle wrote, "Beloved, now are we the sons of God" (1 John 3:2, KJV). In Galatians 3:26-29 Paul made a significant application of sonship as an addition to the line of reasoning that we have been following thus far.

Perhaps the first thing we ought to notice is that beginning with verse 26, Paul changed his viewpoint. We have already seen that in verses 23 to 25 he directed his remarks to Jewish Christians only. One of the ways we know this is that he used the pronouns "we" and "us" so much in those verses. But in verse 26 he switched to "you": "*You* are all sons of God through faith in Christ Jesus," he said, "for all of *you* who were baptized into Christ have clothed *yourselves* with Christ" (verses 26, 27). Paul continued this second-person point of view through to the end of chapter 3 and pretty much through chapter 4, although in chapter 4 he reverted to "we" from time to time.

The question is Whom did he mean by "you"? In the Greek the "you" is plural, just as the first-person "we" and "us" were plural in previous verses. It would seem obvious that Paul was now talking to the Gentile Christians in Galatia. However, right here is where reality may be different from what it appears to be at first glance. In some of his uses of *you* in chapter 4 Paul was unquestionably addressing Gentile Christians only, but not always. Similarly, we cannot assume in chapter 4 that *we* always means Jewish Christians only. In his use of both the first- and the second-person pronouns, he sometimes appears to have been addressing the entire body of Christians in Galatia, Jews and Gentiles together. Context is the determining factor, and we almost have to ask at each use of a pronoun exactly whom Paul had in mind.

Let's return to verse 26. Paul began by saying, "You are all sons of God through faith in Christ Jesus." Was he addressing Gentile Christians only when he said you? There are several clues that he was actually addressing both Jewish and Gentile Christians.

The first clue is the word "all." He said, "You are *all* sons of God through faith in Jesus Christ." The word "all" suggests that Paul meant every

Christian in Galatia, not just the Gentiles. If we were to interpret "you" to mean Gentile Christians only, then we would make him say that only Gentiles were children of God through faith in Christ Jesus. But Paul's whole point thus far has been that the status of being children through blood descent from Abraham, through a relationship to the law, came to an end with Christ. Now through Christ both Jews and Gentiles are children of God.

Paul was obviously responding to the Jewish party's argument that Gentiles could become heirs to salvation only through joining themselves to Judaism. It is true that only the Jews were under the supervision of the law before Christ came, and Gentiles who wanted to become children of God had to become Jews first and place themselves under law. But when Christ came, both Jews and their Gentile proselytes were released from the supervision of the law, and now nobody, Jew or Gentile, needed to approach God through the law. In fact, to do so would be fatal to Christian experience. Paul said, in effect, that the only way for anyone, Jew or Gentile, to be an heir of the promises made to Abraham was to accept Christ: "If you belong to Christ, *then* you are Abraham's seed, and heirs according to the promise." You don't have to be circumcised to be a child of Abraham, for through Christ you become his child directly, bypassing all those laws about circumcision and Temple rituals.

Let's turn now to Galatians 4. Paul continued his "sonship" analogy in this chapter, and he illuminated it with an interesting illustration: "What I am saying is that as long as the heir is a child, he is no different from a slave, although he owns the whole estate. He is subject to guardians and trustees until the time set by his father. So also, when we were children, we were in slavery under the basic principles of the world. But when the time had fully come, God sent his Son, born of a woman, born under law, to redeem those under law, that we might receive the full rights of sons. Because you are sons, God sent the Spirit of his Son into our hearts, the Spirit who calls out, '*Abba*, Father.' So you are no longer a slave, but a son; and since you are a son, God has made you also an heir" (verses 1-7).

Let's break Paul's analogy down into its parts. Four kinds of people are represented: (1) The son while he is still a child, (2) the son after he has become an adult, (3) the slave while he is still a slave, and (4) the slave after he has become a free person. The following diagram suggests how I believe Paul intended us to understand the various parts of this analogy:

The son as a child	The slave as a slave
The Jews before Christ	Gentiles before Christ
The son as an adult	The slave as a freed person
Jewish Christians after Christ	Gentile Christians after Christ

Notice that in verse 3, when he began his explanation of the son/slave analogy, Paul switched back to the first person. He said, "So also, when *we* were children, *we* were in slavery under the basic principles of the world." Who was this "we"? It certainly was not Gentile Christians only. Nowhere in Galatians did Paul ever use the first-person plural to address Gentile Christians. He couldn't have, because "we" includes the person doing the talking, and Paul was not a Gentile. The question is whether he had in mind Jewish Christians only or all Christians in the Galatian churches.

I think he had in mind Jewish Christians only. He said, "When we were *children*, we were in slavery under the basic principles of the world." By "children," he meant the son before he came of age, and that would be the Jews before Christ. The question is Why did he say that "we children" before Christ "were in slavery under the basic principles of the world"? Why didn't he say, "We were in slavery *under the law*"? That would seem to fit the Jews better, and it is one argument in favor of including Gentiles as part of the "we" in this sentence.

Verse 4, however, makes it utterly clear that Paul had in mind Jewish Christians only. He said, "But when the time had fully come, God sent his Son, born of a woman, born under law, *to redeem those under law*, that *we* might receive the full rights of sons." Only of Jewish Christians could it be said that Christ "redeem[ed] those under law." Thus, there is no doubt that in this section of Galatians, when Paul used the plural first-person "we," he meant Jewish Christians only.

The question is Why did Paul say that "we [Jews] were in slavery under the basic principles of the world"? Why didn't he say "We were in slavery under *the law*"?

The answer lies, I think, in what Paul meant by "the basic principles of the world." The expression "basic principles" is a translation of the Greek word *stoicheia* (pronounced stoi-KAY-ah), which means "the basic elements of which the world and the universe are composed"; "in a metaphysical sense, the rudiments of knowledge" (*The SDA Bible Commentary,* vol. 6, p. 965). Paul apparently meant that to know Christ is a higher form of knowledge than either Jews or Gentiles had had before becoming Christians. He was speaking to both Jewish and Gentile Christians, but he was referring to the experience of both Jews and Gentiles *before* Calvary. And to do that he needed a term that would apply to the pre-Christian experience of both. Since the law was not common to both, he chose the expression "basic principles of the world." When applied to the Gentiles, "basic principles of the world" referred to their pagan practices before they became Christians. When applied to the Jews, "basic principles of the world" referred to their status under the law before Christ came. Thus, with one term Paul was able to refer to the pre-Christian time in the lives of both groups.

I believe that when Paul said, "When we were children, we were in slavery under the basic principles of the world," had he been speaking to Jews only, he could have said, "We were in slavery under the law." That would certainly have been true. In fact, it's what he meant. But because his slave/son analogy was about both Jews and Gentiles, he used his new term "basic principles of the world," which was common to both, to refer to the Jews under the law before Christ.

Let's return to the slave/son analogy. Imagine that we can look in on a few minutes in the life of a wealthy Roman landowner. Our friend has both a son and a slave, and one day he orders both of them to weed the garden. The son, who had planned to play with his friend Romeo that day, protests vigorously.

"I'm sorry, but I can't let you go see your friend Romeo today," his father says. "I want you to weed the garden."

You can be sure that Junior weeded the garden alongside the slave that day, regardless of how much he may have wanted to play with Romeo. He could gripe and grumble and groan, but he had to obey his father. He was no better off than the family slave, who could also be ordered to do anything his master wanted him to do.

Yet there was a huge difference between the son and the family slave.

The son was heir to his father's entire estate. Someday he would be out from under his father's authority. Someday the whole estate would be his. The slave had no such hope. He would most likely die a slave to the landowner father.

Like the son, the Jews before Christ were heirs. They still had not "come of age." They were still under the jurisdiction of the law and in one sense no better off than a slave who is not an heir. But when Jesus died on the cross—the point when the son came of age—the Jews were set free of the supervisory function of the law, free of the law as a schoolmaster. As adulthood gave freedom and the full status of sonship to the son, so Christ's first coming gave freedom and the full status of sonship to the Jews.

This raises again the question Was the law before Christ bad? Was it a misfortune to be a Jew before Christ? It almost seems so when we think of the Jews before the cross as slaves. But the whole point of Paul's argument here is that pre-Christian Jews *were* better off than slaves. They *were* better off than Gentiles. They were the heirs! They had "been entrusted with the very words of God" (Rom. 3:2). So Paul didn't think that living under the law was a bad thing. It was only bad to apply after the cross a function of law that came to an end with the cross.

I'd like to use a couple of modern-day analogies.

My son Barry left home in his sophomore year of high school to attend boarding school at Valley Grande Academy in South Texas. Barry enjoyed boarding school. It got him away from home, away from the jurisdiction of Mom and Dad. It gave him more freedom and independence than he'd ever had before. But I can still remember the last semester of his senior year when he called home one night and said, "Dad, the rules around here are terrible. I can't so much as walk out of the dorm at night without telling someone exactly where I'm going and when I'll be back. Can't you get me away from here?"

I said, "Son, you've got only three or four months to go. I can assure you that college will be much different. Just be patient. Stick it out just a little longer."

Barry did wait. (What choice did he have?) A few weeks after he started college I asked him what it was like.

"It's like a breath of fresh air, Dad. It's so wonderful to be in college!"

He could leave the dormitory any time he wanted to, and if he failed to sign out, nobody got after him about it. Barry chose to complete college in five years rather than four, and I never heard him complain about restrictions.

Think for a moment how foolish it would have been for Barry the college student to return to Valley Grande Academy and place himself under its rules and regulations. Nobody in his right mind would do that. Does this mean that the rules at the academy were bad? Of course not! They were very good for high school-age boarding school students. Barry found Valley Grande Academy to be a liberating experience when he first went there. He was much more independent. What glorious freedom he found at the academy—until he discovered, a few years later, that what he had thought to be freedom really wasn't.

Similarly, the law gave the Jews great freedom when they first received it on Sinai. But after 1,500 years it was time to take another step toward even greater freedom in Christ. How foolish it was of the Jewish party to place themselves and Gentile Christians back under the law once they had all "graduated to college"—to a new system based on faith in Jesus.

That's what Paul was saying in Galatians 3 and 4.

Here's another analogy. This one is about an ocean liner. Our ship sails out of New York Harbor and steams toward London. Unfortunately, halfway across the Atlantic Ocean it sinks. Fortunately all the passengers manage to get into lifeboats. The ship's radio officer had sent out an SOS signal as soon as he was informed of the trouble, and within an hour or two a nearby ship comes sailing over and picks up everyone. All the people are safe and happy on the new ship.

Were the lifeboats good for the people when they were floating out there on the Atlantic Ocean? Of course! Those little boats saved their lives. They would have been stupid to jump out of the lifeboats. But once they got into the ship that rescued them, they would have been even more stupid to return to the lifeboats. The little boat that was a lifesaver at one point would have become a death trap a few hours later.

Paul's point in Galatians was that the Jewish party was trying to force Gentile Christians, and indeed themselves, back into a system that had once helped God's people experience salvation but which Christ's death had abolished. It was good before Christ, but it was a death trap after Christ.

In verse 6 Paul said, "Because you are sons . . ." Notice the switch in viewpoint back to *"you."* Was Paul addressing Gentile Christians only, or did he have in mind both Jews and Gentiles? Since he had just finished addressing "we Jews" only, it is again attractive to think that "you" meant

Gentiles only. And in this instance I think that is what he had in mind. The context suggests it, particularly the pronouns.

However, there's something odd about these pronouns. Here is Paul's sentence with the odd pronouns italicized: "Because *you* are sons, God sent the Spirit of his Son into *our* hearts."

Notice that one of these pronouns is in the second-person plural and the other is first-person plural: "Because you [second-person plural] are sons, God sent the Spirit of his Son into our [first-person plural] hearts." Since both pronouns are plural in the Greek, it seems logical to conclude that they referred to separate groups in the Galatian churches. Again our first impulse is to conclude that Paul had Gentile Christians in mind when he said "you" and Jewish Christians when he said "we." And again this first impulse is correct—or so it seems to me. At any rate, let's try interpreting the sentence that way to see if it makes sense.

Paul appears to have said that the Jews couldn't receive the Holy Spirit until the Gentiles had become sons. A paraphrase of his sentence may help to make this point more clear: "It is because you Gentiles are now sons that God is able to send the Spirit of His Son into the hearts of us Jews." Is that really what Paul meant—that the Jews couldn't receive the Holy Spirit until the Gentiles had changed from being slaves to being sons through Christ? I think so, and here's why.

The prophet Joel said that in the last days God's Spirit would be poured out on everyone—not on just a few select prophets, as in Old Testament times, but upon everyone (Joel 2:28, 29). Joel mentioned young men, old men, and—surprise—even young women! But God had an even bigger surprise in store. He planned to pour out His Spirit even on Gentiles!

I think Paul meant that the Spirit could not be poured out on anyone—not even Jews—until He could be poured out on everyone. When the Gentiles were also made children through Christ, and not kept as mere household slaves, that was the signal for the Spirit to be poured out on everyone, including Jews. That's my best guess as to what Paul meant when he said, "Because you [Gentiles] are sons, God sent the Spirit of his Son into our [Jews] hearts." But it is a guess.

In verse 7 Paul said, "So you are no longer a slave, but a son; and since you are a son, God has made you also an heir." Paul was obviously referring to Gentiles here. His slave/son analogy demands that. Before Christ the Jews had no more rights than slaves, but they still were not slaves. They were sons. Only Gentiles were actually slaves in their pre-Christian lives. So in this instance Paul was clearly addressing Gentiles only when he said "you." Before Christ the Jews were no better off than the family slave because they were under the father's jurisdiction. Now, after Christ, the former slaves were just as well off as the son-become-heir because they also had been adopted as children and made full-fledged heirs.

In verse 8 Paul said, "Formerly, when you did not know God, you were slaves to those who by nature are not gods, but now that you know God—or rather are known by God—how is it that you are turning back to those weak and miserable principles?"

Again Paul was obviously talking to the Gentiles, because he used the pronoun "you." He would not have said of the Jews "Formerly when you did not know God." The Jews always knew God. They may have had confused ideas about Him, but they had the true God in mind. It was the Gentiles who did not know the true God.

Next Paul said, "But now that you [Gentiles] know God—or rather are known by God—*how is it that you are turning back to those weak and miserable principles?*" (verse 9). In their pre-Christian lives the Gentile members in Galatia had been pagans. Paul seems to be accusing them of going back to their old pagan practices. But there isn't even a hint in Galatians that the Gentile Christians were returning to their old pagan lifestyle. Paul wrote Galatians to protest that the Gentile Christians were turning to Judaism. What did he mean when he asked, "How is it that you [Gentiles] are turning back to those weak and miserable principles?" when it was Judaism they were turning to, not paganism?

I believe Paul meant that the Gentiles, in turning to Judaism, were adopting a way of life that actually differed very little from their former life as pagans. According to Paul's son/slave analogy, before the son came of age he and the slave were on the same footing. In a very real sense, both Jews and Gentiles were slaves before Christ—the Jews to the law, the Gentiles to paganism. Paul's point was that in submitting to the rituals of Old Testament law, the Gentiles were turning to something that was every bit as much slavery as the condition they had been in when they were pagans.

"Do you wish to be enslaved by them all over again?" Paul asked. "You are observing special days and months and seasons and years! I fear for you, that somehow I have wasted my efforts on you" (verses 9-11). Since "you" meant Gentiles only in the previous sentence, it probably meant the same here. However, the entire body of Galatian believers had fallen under the influence of the Jewish party, not just the Gentiles, so it would also be correct to say that "you" in this sentence meant both Jews and Gentiles.

Paul's reference to "special days" has been used by those who keep Sunday as evidence that keeping the seventh-day Sabbath was done away with in the New Testament. However, Paul didn't say anything about the Sabbath in this verse. To the contrary, he mentioned not only days but also months, seasons, and years—all in the same breath. Throughout our history, the typical Adventist interpretation of this verse has been to deny that it had anything to do with the weekly Sabbath. We have pointed out that the Sabbath of the fourth commandment, the Sabbath of the weekly cycle, could never be associated with other special celebrations, such as months and seasons and years. The seventh-day Sabbath was a part of the Ten Commandments, a part of the moral law, whereas these other celebrations and festivals were all a part of the ceremonial law. The Ten Commandments are eternal principles that were given to the entire human race, whereas the ceremonial law with its festivals was a part of the temple ritual that was given just to the Jews.

This is all true enough, of course. We today do not keep the monthly and yearly festivals that pertained to the Jewish sanctuary ritual. To do so would be to revert to the weak and miserable principles that Paul condemned in the previous verse.

But is that the only valid application of Galatians 4:9, 10 for us today? I wonder whether, by limiting Paul's comments to the ceremonial law, we don't miss the whole point of his argument thus far in Galatians. I wonder if we do not, in fact, revert to the flawed interpretation our pioneers put on the schoolmaster prior to 1888.

You will recall that our traditional explanation of that passage was similar to our explanation of the days, months, seasons, and years. We equated the schoolmaster with the ceremonial law. We did this because it seemed unthinkable to us that the moral law should be limited to the Jewish era of history in any sense.

While his understanding of Galatians 3 was somewhat limited, Waggoner's conclusion that the schoolmaster included the moral law did start us in the right direction. And if the schoolmaster issue in Galatians 3 is the context for our understanding of Galatians 4—which it obviously is—then we need to consider the possibility that the Sabbath of the Ten

Commandments might be included in Paul's comments in 4:10 about days, months, seasons, and years.

One point to notice is that while nearly all Paul's comments thus far in Galatians have been theoretical, this is one of the few places in the letter where he makes a practical application. Yet in saying that, are we looking at Paul's epistle from our own limited point of view? I feel certain that to Paul the entire letter was intensely practical. He was explaining to the Galatian Christians the theological implication of their daily lifestyle. The days, months, seasons, and years happened to be an important part of that lifestyle, and Paul's theological explanation in Galatians 3 applied to that problem.

I believe there is a very appropriate way to include the weekly Sabbath in Paul's remarks in Galatians 4:10—a way that does not in any way diminish our obligation to observe the fourth commandment. Let me assure you right from the start that the issue in this passage is *not* Sabbath versus Sunday, if for no other reason than that there is no evidence anywhere in the New Testament that Sunday observance was an issue for the early Christian church prior to A.D. 100. Nor is the issue whether the Ten Commandments are binding on Christians, because Paul made it utterly clear in Romans that they are. The issue is *how* we keep the commandments.

And this is a lesson that applies to Adventists and our seventh-day Sabbath-keeping as much as it did to New Testament Christians and their observance of both the weekly Sabbath and other Jewish feast days.

The issue is *how* we keep the Sabbath. Do we keep it by the rule book, with our primary attention given to what is right and wrong to *do* on the Sabbath? Or is the primary focus of our Sabbath-keeping a relationship with Jesus and our Christian brothers and sisters? If the former, then Galatians 4:10 applies to the weekly Sabbath as much as it does to any of the yearly Sabbaths, new moons, and other festivals in the Jewish religious year. Sabbath-keeping by the rule book is a reversion to the "weak and miserable" basic principles of the world that Paul spoke about in Galatians 4:9, just before his comments about days and months and seasons and years.

Please do not think that I'm doing away with rules. The Ten Commandments—principles of love—are stated as rules. Rules have a very important place in life, especially for children and those who are young in the Christian faith.

I pointed out in an earlier chapter that parents set down rules for hygiene, punctuality, diet, etc. We say, "Brush your teeth, get to bed by 8:00, and eat your spinach before your dessert." Children need these rules to get them started on good habits. At that stage in life rules to live by are important. But mature adults are not slaves to those rules. They brush their teeth, get to bed on time, and eat their spinach before their dessert because they have learned that doing these things keeps them healthy and happy.

The same can be true of young Christians. Often when I study the Bible with those wanting to learn how to keep the Sabbath, they will ask, "How am I supposed to keep the Sabbath? What should I do? What should I *not* do?" So I tell them: Go to church, don't go to your job, and don't do your housework and yard work. Early in their Christian experience these guidelines are helpful in establishing good Sabbath-keeping habits. But I try to make it clear to all my students that their objective in observing these rules should be to make the "laws" so much a part of life that they can ultimately forget about the regulations and concentrate on the real purpose of the Sabbath, which is to enhance their relationship with God and other Christians.

If Paul had in mind the weekly Sabbath in Galatians 4:10, he was not telling his readers to stop keeping the day, nor was he telling them to switch days. Neither was he telling them that Sunday is the Christian sabbath and observance of the seventh-day Sabbath is a reversion to "those weak and miserable principles." In fact, he wasn't even telling them that rules are bad. He was telling the Galatian Christians to move beyond the rules and regulations to the heart of what it means to keep the Sabbath.

Paul said, "I fear for you, that somehow I have wasted my efforts on you." Poor Paul! How terrible he must have felt. After spending all that time and effort leading these Gentile converts to freedom in Christ, and leading the Jewish converts to accept them in Christ, a group of dissidents had come into the Galatian church and led them off into apostasy.

Next he said, "I plead with you brothers" (verse 12). Earlier he had said, "You foolish Galatians! Who has bewitched you?" (Gal. 3:1). That sounds an awful lot like condemnation. But Paul wasn't condemning these people. He loved them. What sounded like condemnation was actually a plea for them to remain faithful to the truth.

"I plead with you, brothers," he said, "become like me, for I became like you" (verse 12). Paul probably meant that he wanted his Gentile friends to become free like him in the gospel. When Jesus set him free, he gave up his

Judaism to become like Gentiles who had never been under the law, and he was inviting his Gentile friends to become like him—free of both paganism and Jewish legalism. He said something similar to this in 1 Corinthians 9:19-23: "Though I am free and belong to no man, I make myself a slave to everyone, to win as many as possible. To the Jews I became like a Jew, to win the Jews. To those under the law I became like one under the law . . . so as to win those under the law. *To those not having the law [Gentiles] I became like one not having the law . . . so as to win those not having the law.* To the weak I became weak, to win the weak. I have become all things to all men so that by all possible means I might save some. I do all this for the sake of the gospel, that I may share in its blessings."

"You have done me no wrong," Paul continued. "As you know, it was because of an illness that I first preached the gospel to you" (Gal. 4:12, 13). Nowhere did either Paul, or Luke writing in the book of Acts, tell us how, when, or where Paul became ill. There is some speculation that he came down with a disease in the lowlands of Asia Minor, perhaps near the Mediterranean Sea, and moved temporarily to Galatia, which was a higher region, to recover. Whatever the details, it was an illness that first brought Paul to the region of Galatia. And always the missionary, even though he was ill, he preached Christ, won some of the Galatian citizens to the faith, and established a church.

Then Paul said, "Even though my illness was a trial to you, you did not treat me with contempt or scorn. Instead, you welcomed me as if I were an angel of God, as if I were Christ Jesus himself" (verse 14). This shows the love these people had for Paul. Anytime people are experiencing a burden and yet enjoy it, that's an indication that they have been converted. Even though Paul's illness was a trial to these new Christians, they did not treat him with contempt or scorn. Rather, they welcomed him as if he were an angel of God, or even Jesus Christ Himself. These people were obviously converted.

"What has happened to all your joy?" Paul asked (verse 15). The Jewish party was trying to get the Gentile Christians back into slavery, back into a joyless Christianity. The Galatians had been so happy in the Lord. They had even found it a joy to take care of Paul when he was a burden to them. "What happened to that joy?" Paul asked.

The problem with legalism is that it removes joy. If my son had gone back to Valley Grande Academy, he would have lost all the joy that he found in college.

"I can testify," Paul said, "that, if you could have done so, you would have torn out your eyes and given them to me" (verse 15). Apparently Paul had eye trouble. Perhaps he never fully recovered from the blindness that he experienced on the Damascus road.

In verse 17 Paul said, "Those people are zealous to win you over, but for no good." This is an obvious reference to the Jewish party.

Have you ever seen a zealous fanatic? People like that are always trying to win over converts from the main body of believers to their particular cause, to their brand of theology and lifestyle. Have you ever seen that happen in the Seventh-day Adventist Church? Have you ever seen it happen in your local Adventist congregation to someone you brought into the faith? If so, perhaps you can more easily understand Paul's deep concern for the Gentile Christians in Galatia. The Jewish party was zealous to win over his converts, but for no good.

"What they want is to alienate you from us, so that you may be zealous for them" (verse 17). Again, does that sound familiar? There are many good independent ministries serving the Adventist Church. The leaders of these ministries take a positive attitude toward the church and encourage their supporters to remain faithful to the main body of believers. A few, however, seem to thrive on alienating people from the church. They create suspicion and doubt, and siphon off people to join them in their criticism. These disaffected souls then pour money and energy into the critic's "cause," which, of course, is what the critic is after. Like the Jewish party, these critics "alienate you from us [the church as a whole], so that you may be zealous *for them.*"

So often the hidden motive behind this kind of behavior is pride. "It is fine to be zealous, provided the purpose is good," Paul said, "and to be so always and not just when I am with you" (verse 18). Anyone who reads the literature put out by these critical independent ministries, who listens to their audio tapes or watches their videotapes, immediately senses an intense zeal. The critic claims to love the church and have only its best interest at heart. But it takes only a few moments of reading, listening, or watching to detect that that zeal is "for no good." It is, instead, critical and destructive.

Another thing I've noticed about many of these zealous independent ministries is their fascination with standards. Their main burden seems to be to point out the flaws in everyone else. Again, please don't think I mean that standards are bad. We all need them. The problem with these independent ministries and the people who join them is that standards seem to be the major focus of their religion, the chief way by which they judge whether others are Christians. Anytime we allow rules and regulations about lifestyle to become the focus of our religion, we have fallen into the trap of the Jewish party, even if we are not insisting on their particular laws.

And now comes one of the most caring statements in the whole book of Galatians, which helps us understand Paul's real motive for writing to the Galatian Christians: "My dear children, for whom I am again in the pains of childbirth until Christ is formed in you, how I wish I could be with you now and change my tone, because I am perplexed about you!" (verses 19, 20). Suddenly the apparent harshness in Paul's language earlier in Galatians vanishes. He loved these people. He wasn't trying to condemn them. He was deeply concerned about their spiritual life. He feared that they might lose the joy and freedom in Christ that they had learned from him. That, in a nutshell, is what Galatians is all about. It's the message that all of us, in whatever age we may live, can take from Galatians and apply to our own hearts.

Never exchange the joy and freedom that you have in Christ for a joyless religion that is centered on rules and regulations!

CHAPTER 14

New Versus Old Covenant
Galatians 4:21-31

I n this chapter we will examine another of those passages that
have troubled Seventh-day Adventists for many years. The passage does not refer to the law as such, except in the first verse,
where it refers to the entire Pentateuch (a point that I will explain shortly). The problem with the passage is that it speaks of
Sinai in a rather disparaging way. Since the Ten Commandments,
which we cherish, came from Sinai, any unfavorable remarks about Sinai
tend to make the Ten Commandments appear in a bad light.

Here's the passage we will be considering in this chapter:

"Tell me, you who want to be under the law, are you not aware of
what the law says? For it is written that Abraham had two sons, one by the
slave woman and the other by the free woman. His son by the slave
woman was born in the ordinary way; but his son by the free woman was
born as the result of a promise.

"These things may be taken figuratively, for the women represent two
covenants. One covenant is from Mount Sinai and bears children who are
to be slaves: This is Hagar. Now Hagar stands for Mount Sinai in Arabia
and corresponds to the present city of Jerusalem, because she is in slavery
with her children. But the Jerusalem that is above is free, and she is our
mother. For it is written:

"'Be glad, O barren woman, who bears no children; break forth and
cry aloud, you who have no labor pains; because more are the children of
the desolate woman than of her who has a husband.'

"Now you, brothers, like Isaac, are children of promise. At that time
the son born in the ordinary way persecuted the son born by the power of
the Spirit. It is the same now. But what does the Scripture say? 'Get rid of
the slave woman and her son, for the slave woman's son will never share
in the inheritance with the free woman's son.' Therefore, brothers, we are
not children of the slave woman, but of the free woman" (Gal. 4:21-31).

The question is What did Paul mean by his analogy of the slave woman and the free woman, Sinai, and the two Jerusalems? Let's begin with verse 21: "Tell me, you who want to be under the law."

Who is this "you"? I think it refers to any Christian in Galatia, whether Jew or Gentile, who was being influenced by the Jewish party. Paul had taught all of them that the function of law that God planned for His people before the cross did not apply to Christians after the cross. Unfortunately, the Jewish party had turned some of the Galatian Christians from this principle, making them "want" to submit to the Old Testament function of law again.

Having referred to the law, you'd think Paul would follow this up with a comment about the law from Exodus, Leviticus, or Deuteronomy, but he didn't. Instead, he told the story of Abraham, Hagar, and Sarah, which is found in Genesis. What did he mean, then, when he said "You who want to be under the law, are you not aware of what the law says?" Is Genesis "the law"?

Yes. The Jews considered the law to include not only the books of Exodus, Leviticus, and Deuteronomy, but the entire Pentateuch—the first five books of the Bible. So Paul quite appropriately, according to Jewish thinking, referred to the story of Abraham as "the law." This is one of the clues that the churches in Galatia were probably made up of a high percentage of Jews. Paul would not have been as likely to use a Jewish way of speaking about the law had a large majority of his readers been Gentiles with little background in Jewish thought patterns.

Now let's look at the story. "It is written that Abraham had two sons, one by the slave woman and the other by the free woman. His son by the slave woman was born in the ordinary way; but his son by the free woman was born as a result of a promise" (verses 22, 23).

Paul did not seem to be concerned here by the fact that Ishmael's birth came about through Abraham's distrust of God. He didn't say that Ishmael was born in a sinful way. He said that Ishmael was born "in the ordinary way." The King James Version says "after the flesh"—that is, in the way human beings are usually born. Paul's emphasis was not on the moral implication of Abraham's act in having a child by Hagar, but on the legal status of the two mothers and their sons. One mother and son were slaves, and the other mother and son were free.

Paul's point was that Ishmael was conceived the way babies are normally conceived—by a man and a woman of childbearing age coming together in sexual intercourse. Isaac, on the other hand, was born long after Sarah had passed the age when a woman can bear children. Isaac's birth came about through a miracle. God kept His promise that Abraham and Sarah would have a son by making it possible for the infertile Sarah to bear a son. Thus, Isaac was a son of promise. And here, of course, we get back to the theme of Galatians—that righteousness came to Abraham by a promise, not by law. The two boys and their mothers are simply an analogy of this theme. One of the women was a slave, and by law her son was also a slave. The other woman was free, and she gave birth to a son who legally was also free.

Next Paul said, "These things may be taken figuratively, for the women represent two covenants" (verse 24). This is not the only place where the Bible talks about two covenants. Jeremiah said that God would make "a new covenant with the house of Israel" (Jer. 31:31). The author of Hebrews explained that by calling Jeremiah's covenant "new," God had "made the first one obsolete" (Heb. 8:13).

It would be easy to suppose that in his analogy of Sinai and the two women and their sons Paul had in mind the covenants that Jeremiah and the author of Hebrews spoke about, but I think this would be a mistake. According to the explanation of Jeremiah's two covenants in the book of Hebrews, a day was coming (Christ's day) when God would make a new covenant with the house of Israel because there was something wrong with the old covenant. There is a significant difference between that and what Paul said in Galatians. Nowhere in Galatians did Paul suggest that there was anything wrong with the Jewish religion prior to Calvary. To the contrary, he seems to have had a high regard for that system for its own time. Hebrews, on the other hand, clearly says that there was something wrong with the first covenant, and it goes on to say that the fault lay with the people—that is, the Israelites (see Heb. 8:7, 8). Thus, to a certain extent we are comparing apples with oranges when we try to let Paul's discussion of the two covenants in Galatians enlighten our understanding of the two covenants in Hebrews or vice versa. For this reason, I'm going to discuss the two covenants in Galatians without reference to the discussion of covenants in Hebrews.

Paul said that Hagar and her son represent "the present city of Jerusalem, because she is in slavery with her children" (Gal. 4:25). He had already talked about slavery in Galatians. You will recall that earlier in chapter 4 he compared the son who was an heir with the slave who had no rights. In this analogy, the son represented the Jews before Calvary and the slave represented Gentiles before they accepted Christ. However, in his Sarah-Hagar analogy, it is the Jews who are slaves. Hagar, the slave woman, represents "the present city of Jerusalem." It was Jews who were trying to relate to God after Christ the same way they related to Him before Christ.

The people in the Old Testament did not think of their religion as slavery, to be sure, nor did God intend that they should. But after Christ came, any effort to remain in Judaism was slavery, the same as an older son trying to return to the jurisdiction of his father as though he were a child, the same as my son, after graduating from academy and going to college, trying to put himself under the old academy rules.

It is attractive to suppose that in comparing Hagar with the Jerusalem of his day Paul had in mind the Jewish legalism so pervasive at Christ's time, which distorted the law God gave at Sinai. Christ vigorously opposed this legalism, and no doubt Paul would have called this slavery also. But here, as elsewhere in Galatians, Paul had in mind the revelation that God gave at Sinai as something good for His people at that time. Yet even the most pure form of Judaism, which was such a great blessing to God's people before Christ, was slavery to remain in after Christ had come. Hagar represented Christians who believed that it was necessary for Christians to place themselves under the jurisdiction of law the way God's people did in the Old Testament.

Sarah, on the other hand, "represents the Jerusalem that is above," Paul said, "and she is our mother" (verse 26). In this short sentence Paul included all Christians, whether Jew or Gentile, whether in Galatia or anywhere else, who have accepted the freedom from Judaism that Christ and Christianity brought. He meant all Christians who accept salvation without submitting to Jewish Temple rituals and circumcision. In our day this means all Christians who have a high regard for biblical standards but do not make standards the basis of their religious experience.

With the analogy of the slave woman and the free woman, Paul concluded his basic theological thrust against the Jewish party. We will look briefly at verses 28-31 in a moment, but first I would like to take a moment to think about everything that we have discussed up to this point in Galatians and how it applies to us today.

One practical lesson is this: Don't go back to whatever God has called you out of. There is a passage in Revelation that I think applies here. Writing to the Christians in Ephesus, God, through John, said: "I hold this against you: You have forsaken your first love" (Rev. 2:4). Here was a church that went back. When God has given you victory over sin, stay with it. This doesn't mean you'll never commit that sin again, but whatever spiritual lesson you learned that gave you the victory the first time, stay with it. Keep trying it, and keep working with it, keep on cooperating with Jesus and the Holy Spirit. Don't give up and say, "I guess I can't conquer that sin after all." When God gives you a special spiritual experience with Himself, keep doing whatever it was that brought you to that point in the first place.

To do otherwise is to be among the five foolish virgins, who lost their eternal life because they did not keep their lamps burning. I think we can safely say that the five foolish virgins represent those who failed to take Paul's advice in Galatians. They started out with their lights burning bright. They were truly converted Christians. But as time went by, they slipped back. They went back to a former experience.

How did the wise virgins continue to grow instead of going back? They continued in daily prayer and daily study of the Word. They continued in regular fellowship with God's people. They took advantage of every opportunity to share with others what God had done for them. They cultivated the presence of the Holy Spirit in their lives. That's how they avoided going back. That's how you and I can keep from going back.

In Galatians 3:1 Paul said, "You foolish Galatians! Who has bewitched you? Before your very eyes Jesus Christ was clearly portrayed as crucified. I would like to learn just one thing from you: Did you receive the Spirit by observing the law, or by believing what you heard?" Paul placed a great emphasis on the presence of the Holy Spirit in people's lives. And he said, "Don't go back. You received the Holy Spirit by believing what you heard; don't go back now and try and receive the Holy Spirit by what you do."

Genuine Christians assume that their Christian experience tomorrow will be ahead of what it is today. Genuine Christians go in search of tomorrow's experience. They continually ask God for more change of heart, for more victory over bad habits and sins. The only guarantee for not going back is to continue going forward. That is one of the most important lessons we can learn from Paul's letter to the Galatians.

Another lesson we today can learn from Galatians is to avoid legalism. I've already discussed that somewhat in previous chapters, and the next chapter will go into this question even more. However, in Galatians 4:28-31 Paul advised his readers how to deal with legalistic Christians. He said in verses 28-31: "Now you, brothers, like Isaac, are children of promise. At that time the son born in the ordinary way persecuted the son born by the power of the Spirit." The Jewish party was literally persecuting the Christians in Galatia by trying to bring them into the slavery of Judaism.

We today sometimes face the same problem—people who force their standards on us, who judge us harshly if we don't live just the way they think we should. That is precisely what the Jewish party was trying to do to the Gentile Christians in Galatia. They were trying to throw a guilt trip on them. In our zeal to protect the church from corruption, it's important that each of us guards against trying to force others to live the way we think they should. We must avoid judging them harshly when they don't practice the Christian life the way we do. If you find yourself frequently complaining about people in the church who lower the standards and if you find yourself bewailing the downward drift of the church, then watch out. You may be a legalist persecuting other Christians. Your greatest need is to let God take care of His own church. Give these people the freedom to live their lives the way *they* think they should, even if it's not the way *you* think they should.

Does that mean the church should not be concerned about the way people live? Of course not. Paul came down hard on sinful behavior. Read 1 Corinthians 5 if you don't think so. But in matters of dress, diet, entertainment, Sabbathkeeping, and other lifestyle standards, I am convinced that the less advice we give others, the better, except when we are asked. We only alienate them when we do.

I heard recently of a church elder who makes himself the guardian of the purity of the church. If someone does something on the Sabbath that is wrong by his standards, or comes to church wearing a piece of jewelry that he considers inappropriate, within a week that person will find a letter in his or her mailbox advising him or her of the sin. Each year this man goes over the nominating committee report with a fine-tooth comb to be sure that every candidate for church office conforms to his personal standards.

Notice how Paul said we should deal with this problem: "But what does the Scripture say? 'Get rid of the slave woman and her son, for the slave woman's son will never share in the inheritance with the free woman's son'" (verse 30). That's pretty tough advice, but it's right to the point. Paul told the Galatian Christians to get rid of the Jewish party. Have nothing more to do with them, he commanded. Send them packing. I don't think Paul meant that the Gentile Christians should be rude to the members of the Jewish party, but he did intend that they be firm—very firm.

Today if someone is trying to send you on a guilt trip because of something you do that he or she doesn't think you should do, follow Paul's advice and "get rid of the slave woman and her son." You don't have to be rude. But you should be firm. You might say something like "Thank you for your advice, but I think I'll let God be my judge on that."

Several years ago I was pastoring a church in Texas, and a couple of men began attending from time to time. These men were members of a small offshoot—a rigid, harsh, legalistic organization. At first they were kind and tactful, but I knew who they were and the kind of trouble they were capable of creating. So I said to them, "Gentlemen, you are welcome to attend my church as long as you understand that this is a Seventh-day Adventist church. You were once Seventh-day Adventists, and you know what we believe. When you make a comment in the Sabbath school class, I expect you to stay basically in line with what Adventists teach. I don't want you upsetting my members with your unique doctrines."

"Oh, yes, pastor," they said, "we'll do that." And for a number of months they did. Then one day one of them stood up and made quite a long speech during a testimony service we were having, and it was not in harmony with the instructions that I had given him. I went to him after the church service and said, "Brother, the speech you made today was out of line with the instructions I gave you, and I'm going to have to ask you not to speak like that in this church again."

He replied, "I will say what the Holy Spirit tells me to say."

I said, "The Bible says that the spirits of the prophets are under the control of the prophets [see 1 Cor. 14:32], and you can control what you say. I don't want you talking like that in this church again."

The man attacked me verbally. Several of my members were present. At that point I had to say to this man and his friend, "I don't want you to come back to this church again, ever." It's not in my nature as a pastor to tell people that they cannot come to my church, but I felt that I had to deal promptly and firmly with this disruption.

For a long time they didn't come back. Then one Sabbath one of my deacons reported to me that they were at the door. "They're trying to get in," he said. "You'd better come and deal with them."

So I went outside and said, "Gentlemen, I thought I instructed you not to come back."

"We thought you weren't going to be here today."

"Well, I am here today," I replied, "and I don't want you in this church. I meant what I said."

To their credit, they both were quite cooperative and left.

I believe I dealt with that situation according to Paul's advice to the Galatian Christians: "Get rid of the slave woman and her son." I was not rude to these men, but I got rid of them.

Does this mean that there is no place for a member going to another member and advising him or her about a fault? After all, doesn't Matthew 18 tell us to point out a sin that we see in another person? How can we tell the difference between the person who is genuinely pointing out a fault and someone who is being a legalist? Let's look at what I think may be some helpful guidelines.

First, the person who is truly practicing Matthew 18 will discuss a clear-cut sin from Scripture, not a personal opinion. Second, he or she will come to you privately and talk to you kindly, without condemnation. Third, the person who comes to you in the mode of Matthew 18 will in all probability talk to you about one thing only. Finally, that person will not keep harassing you day after day, week after week, about this particular problem. Having pointed it out, he or she will leave the follow-up to you. The individual won't talk to others about it and won't make a public issue about it in the church.

If the sin is a serious moral infraction such as adultery or gross dishonesty, you should begin by talking to that person privately. If he or she refuses to listen to you, you should take one or two others with you, and only at that point, if he or she refuses to listen to the advice of several Christians, should you take the problem to the church as a whole.

Two important lessons, then, that I learn from Paul's letter to the Galatians are (1) Don't go back, and (2) don't allow a legalist to harass you. Paul's whole letter to the Galatians is worth these two pieces of practical advice.

CHAPTER 15

Legalism

et's begin this chapter with a short quiz. On a separate sheet of paper write a column of numbers from 1 to 10, and then answer the following questions either yes or no:

1. I'm concerned about the increasing worldliness in the church, especially as seen in the lowering of standards by so many of our members.

2. I have friends who are also concerned about this, and we discuss it quite often.

3. I wish somehow God could use me to bring the church back to its original purity.

4. I feel that some ministers put too much emphasis on righteousness by faith and not enough on obedience.

5. Sometimes I wonder how members who wear jewelry, do wrong things on the Sabbath, attend theaters, and do other worldly things can have a relationship with Jesus.

6. The Bible and Spirit of Prophecy seem so plain about our standards that you wonder sometimes if people have even read them.

7. I'm concerned enough about these people that I have encouraged some of them to be faithful, or I have thought maybe I ought to.

8. I try hard to bring up my children to follow the standards given us by the pioneers. (Or "I wish more parents would bring up their children to follow the standards of the pioneers.")

9. Sometimes I wish there were a way I could make our members obey the standards, and I sure do wonder why the church can't take a firmer stand.

10. I try to encourage my older children (or youth in general, if you have no children) to be faithful to what I taught them.

Near the end of this chapter I'll say a few more words about this quiz, but for now I'd like to depart from our study of Galatians and spend some time discussing legalism. This will help us better understand the last two chapters of Galatians when we come to them.

The word "legalism" has come to have several shades of meaning among Christians. The difference between these various meanings of legalism was illustrated to me several months ago when I read an article in a magazine published by a group of Seventh-day Adventists who operate a spiritual ministry independent of the denomination. The subject of the article was legalism, and the author's main point was that people are unfair when they call him and those who believe as he does legalists. Legalism, he said, is the effort to obtain salvation by keeping the law, and he said that he and his friends don't believe in that. They believe in salvation by grace alone, through faith, apart from any works of the law. Obedience and conformance to standards come as a *result* of salvation, he said, not as a *cause* of salvation.

This author's definition of legalism is one of the correct meanings of the word. By this definition, he and those who believe as he does are not legalists. Every Christian needs this understanding of the relationship between law and grace.

There are, however, other forms of legalism, some of which we see in the church today and some of which we do not see. The Jewish party's form of legalism is one of those that no longer exists among Christians. Here in this book we have examined their theology and Paul's response to it. This type of legalism died with the destruction of Jerusalem in A.D. 70. Another form of legalism is that of the Roman Catholic Church, which developed during the Middle Ages. This form of legalism no longer exists among Protestants.

However, legalism is not just a theology. More fundamentally, it is a set of attitudes—a way of thinking about sin and the relationship of sinners to God and each other. These attitudes have existed in all branches of Christendom from the earliest days of the Christian church to the present. The theology that grows out of this way of thinking will differ from one group of Christians to another, but the attitudes behind these various theologies are common to all forms of legalism. In this chapter we will examine these attitudes that lie at the foundation of legalism.

I think I am safe in saying that these attitudes tend to be most common among conservative Christians—what we sometimes call "fundamentalist" Christianity. Some of them are also evident in the fundamentalist forms of Islam. Much of what I say in this chapter will be typical of legalism among conservative Protestants today, and since I am writing from a Seventh-day Adventist perspective, all of what I say will be typical of Seventh-day Adventist legalism. I will be defining a dozen or more attitudes, all of which I will summarize under three general headings.

Attitudes About Sin and Salvation

In the introduction to his letter to the Galatians, Paul pointed out that the root of the Jewish party's heresy was their incorrect understanding of the gospel. He called it "a different gospel—which is really no gospel at all" (Gal. 1:6, 7). A misunderstanding of the gospel has been the source of all legalism in the Christian church from Paul's time to the present.

The theology of most non-Christian religions is based on the idea that salvation—eternal life beyond the grave—depends on a person's good behavior. Christianity is unique in its teaching that salvation is by grace alone through faith, apart from anything the sinner does. However, the human desire to do something to merit salvation is so strong that it still crops up from time to time among Christians, creating subtle forms of legalism even among those who profess to believe in salvation by grace alone through faith.

The relationship of justification and Christian growth—Adventists almost universally affirm their belief in salvation by grace alone through faith. Our problem tends to be in understanding the relationship of this teaching to character development. This difficulty is perhaps most succinctly illustrated by a statement a man made to me once: "God saves us *from* our sins, not *in* our sins." Legalists of this variety agree that God accepts sinners just as they are when they first come to Christ. He does not require them to overcome certain sins or reach a particular level of character development before He will save them.

But what does God do about the sins that Christians commit after they have been forgiven and have experienced conversion? This is where the "God saves us *from* our sins, not *in* our sins" theology takes over. The idea is that the power of Christ is sufficient to give Christians the victory over every known sin (see Phil. 4:13). Therefore, once people have been converted, perfect performance is not only possible but necessary in order to retain the assurance of salvation. The moment people sin, they break their relationship with Jesus, so the theory goes, and that relationship is not restored until they confess their sins and ask for forgiveness. Sin and justification become an on-off switch for salvation. Justification turns salvation on, and committing a known sin turns it off.

A behavioral definition of sin—At the bottom of this misunderstanding of the gospel, I believe, is an incorrect definition of sin—the idea that sin is what we do (behavior) rather than what we are (the heart). There is quite a debate going on in the Adventist Church over this question, so perhaps we should take a bit of time to clarify the issue.

Saying that sin is primarily what we are, not what we do, does not mean that sinful behavior is inconsequential. The Bible condemns both sinful deeds and the sinful heart. The question is Which is the source of the problem? If the source of the problem is our behavior, then the heart is pure until it is defiled by a person's first sin. By this definition of sin, if a baby could somehow avoid committing that first sin, it would remain sinless and presumably would not need salvation. On the other hand, if the heart is the source of the problem, then every human being is a sinner from the moment of birth, even before one can commit a first sin. We cannot help doing evil things, because the heart, the source of all behavior, is defiled.

The Bible says that all of us are "by nature objects of wrath" (Eph. 2:3). "Surely I was sinful at birth," the psalmist wrote, "sinful from the time my mother conceived me" (Ps. 51:5). Sin is not so much what we *do*. At its foundation, sin is what we *are*. We do sinful deeds because we have sinful hearts. "From within," Jesus said, *"out of men's hearts,* come evil thoughts, sexual immorality, theft, murder, adultery, greed, malice, deceit, lewdness, envy, slander, arrogance and folly. *All these evils come from inside and make a man unclean"* (Mark 7:20-23).

Clearly, then, sin is not so much what we *do*. At its foundation, sin is what we *are*. We do sinful deeds because we have sinful hearts.

This issue has everything to do with legalism. For legalists, who think of sin primarily as behavior, the major objective in Christian growth is to stop doing sinful things. It seems impossible to them that people should consider themselves Christians as long as they continue doing bad things.

However, if sin is primarily what we are on the inside, and only secondarily what we do, then the solution to the problem is first of all to change the heart. We call this conversion. Behavior change may not occur instantly following conversion, but it will happen in time. An evil character develops gradually out of the motives of an evil heart. When the heart is changed, gradual character development in the other direction begins.

The question—the whole point of the debate—is this: If behavior change happens only gradually following conversion, what is our standing with God during the time we are struggling with temptation, before victory is complete? Legalists find it extremely difficult, if not impossible, to believe that God will accept sinners—sins and all—during the victory process. They insist that "God saves us *from* our sins, not *in* our sins."

However, it is my personal conviction that as long as we choose to keep our relationship with Jesus we retain our conversion during the time that victory is in process, before it is complete. I absolutely reject the on-off switch theory that justification turns salvation on and every subsequent sin turns it off until it is confessed, at which point justification turns it back on again. I believe that God accepts us with our character defects and the wrong behaviors that spring from them, as long as we maintain our relationship with Him. The way to turn off salvation is not by sinning, but by rebelling, by refusing even to be interested in salvation or in living the Christian life. Sadly, that is probably more often done by neglect than by conscious choice.

It would perhaps be too much to say that everyone who adopts the behavioral view of sin that I have described is a legalist. However, I believe this definition of sin is a setup for legalistic ways of thinking.

A behavioral definition of perfection—A behavioral definition of perfection arises naturally out of a behavioral definition of sin. If sin is primarily what we do, then perfection is also primarily what we do. Accordingly, growth toward perfection is a matter of learning which behaviors are wrong and obtaining the power of Christ to overcome them. Ultimate perfection is reaching the point where one no longer does wrong things—sinlessness.

There is, of course, a great truth in the idea that perfection has to do with behavior. The Ten Commandments were stated primarily in behavioral terms. No perfect person will commit adultery or cheat or lie. But if sinful behavior arises out of an evil heart, then the real cure to the sin problem lies not in changing the behavior, but in changing the heart. Wrong behavior is simply a flag that is waving in front of our faces, warning us that we still have a sinful heart. At its foundation, perfection is primarily a condition of the heart and only secondarily a condition of one's behavior.

This is a crucial point of theology for any eschatological community (a group of Christians who are preparing for earth's final events) that believes, as Seventh-day Adventists do, in the perfection of God's end-time people.

I do not have a problem with the idea that God's end-time people will be as perfect as God can make human beings this side of the second coming of Christ. The book of Revelation seems to suggest that (see Rev. 7:1-8; 14:1-5, 12; 16:15). However, it is utterly essential for any community of Christians that holds this belief to have a correct understanding of sin and salvation. Otherwise, with their efforts to be perfect, they are in great danger of driving themselves and others to spiritual insanity, continually checking up on their own behavior and everyone else's when the real problem is the heart. This is legalism at its absolute worst.

An obsession with standards—The behavioral concept of sin and perfection that I just described, together with our belief in end-time perfection, lie at the foundation of much of the legalism I have observed in the Adventist Church. If sin is primarily what we do (rather than what we are on the inside) and if perfection is measured in terms of behavior (rather than of the heart), then it becomes of paramount importance to find out which behaviors are right and which are wrong. Righteousness becomes a long list of do's and don'ts, with a continual search for more. And lifestyle standards fit into this requirement like a hand fits a glove.

Many of the legalists I know have an obsession with lifestyle and standards of behavior. And because it's not just them but a whole community of saints that God is perfecting for the end time, they frequently make an issue about people in the church who wear jewelry, attend the theater, do certain things on the Sabbath, etc. In one Adventist community where I used to live was a group that met regularly to check up on each other's character development and to point out each other's flaws. One of their primary motives for meeting apparently was to help each other prepare for the end time.

A measure of Christian experience—Arising out of this obsession with standards is another attitude that is closely related to it. Legalists tend to put a great emphasis on lifestyle standards as a measure of progress in the Christian life. When they see a woman in the church wearing earrings and a necklace, their first thought is that she must be slipping in her Christian experience. But she may have considered the matter prayerfully from Scripture and decided that God does not object to what she is doing.

We must allow each other this freedom as Christians. The point is that it's nobody else's business. We wouldn't make it our business to judge a woman about the type of clothing she wore to church. We wouldn't say that the woman who wore a dress was a good Christian but the woman sitting in the pew beside her was losing her relationship with Jesus because she wore a skirt and blouse. Why should we pass judgment on a person's Christian experience because of earrings and a necklace?

"But the church has a standard," you say. "We don't wear jewelry."

That's true, and I'm not arguing that we abandon our standard on jewelry. Standards aren't legalism. I have no problem with anyone who chooses not to wear jewelry, and I have no problem with a group of people (a church) agreeing not to use jewelry for adornment. But I do have a problem with people using this as a basis for judging the quality of one another's Christian experience. *That's* legalism.

Rejection of sinners—At its most unfortunate extreme, the tendency of legalists to misunderstand the gospel sometimes leads them to reject people who have sinned. Somehow, being kind to the sinner is tantamount in their minds to condoning his or her sin. This attitude, which was rife among certain Pharisees of Christ's day (see Luke 15:1, 2), often leads to some of the worst forms of social cruelty, and all in the name of keeping the church pure!

The Bible as a Rulebook

If righteousness is measured primarily in terms of behavior, then obviously it's important to find out which behaviors are right and which are wrong. The main source for such information, of course, is the Bible. Seventh-day Adventists also view the writings of Ellen White as authoritative, which makes her a source of authority for us about right and wrong behavior. The legalist, intent on discovering right and wrong behavior, will take every inspired statement about behavior as a command that is to be literally obeyed for all time.

This desire for an authoritative statement for all behavior leads to some unfortunate consequences.

Difficulty making personal moral decisions—Their need for an inspired definition of right and wrong behavior often makes it difficult for legalists to exercise their own judgment about moral issues. They would rather be told what is the right course of action than to decide for themselves.

Scripture does, of course, point out certain behaviors that are right and others that are wrong, as does Ellen White. But even more important is the Bible's description of the heart that is right with God and the heart that is not. And in this context the Bible does not so much define right and wrong behavior as it does right and wrong motive, often leaving the determination of what is appropriate behavior up to the individual.

But legalists find the idea of making up their own minds about what is right and wrong quite threatening. This is particularly true when common sense would suggest a course of action contrary to what Scripture seems to say. For example, Adventists keep the Sabbath on Saturday, and we try to keep it in harmony with the biblical principle of avoiding common business dealings on the Sabbath. Many Adventists, myself included, observe this principle by filling the car with gas on Friday and avoiding eating out at a restaurant on the Sabbath. However, if I am obliged to drive several hours on the Sabbath, I'll buy gas with a clear conscience, and if I find myself away from home with no place to eat, I'll buy food on the Sabbath. Not only would some legalists have a hard time doing that, but they would also condemn anyone who did.

Turning cultural statements into timeless practices—Another trait that is common among legalists is the tendency to make a standard for all time out of scriptural statements that were almost certainly intended for the culture to which they were written. Let me illustrate.

A friend of mine who spent a number of years in the Far East told me that in the Thai culture children show respect for their elders by putting their hands together below the chin and bowing. Suppose that the apostle Paul had been giving advice to children of the modern Thai culture. He would surely have said, "Children, fold your hands and bow to your elders." A correct interpretation of this hypothetical inspired statement would lead us to understand that children in every culture should show respect for their elders in whatever way their culture shows respect, whether it be bowing, or saying Mr. and Mrs., or "Yes, Sir" and "Yes, Ma'am." However, had Paul actually said this, 2,000 years later Christian legalists around the world would have elevated this custom of the Thai culture to an eternal form of divinely mandated behavior and would instruct their children that God wanted them to fold their hands and bow as a way of showing respect.

That is, in fact, what has happened with certain biblical statements that are clearly cultural. For example, I know of a number of men who refuse to trim their beards because of a certain prohibition in Leviticus 19:27. We do not know why God gave this command to the Israelites, but it almost certainly had to do with some practice of that time. It may be that trimming the beard was a common religious practice of the Canaanites and that God wanted His people to show themselves distinct from that religion. He did *not* mean that trimming one's beard is forever and always wrong!

I used to know a man who believed that it was wrong to wear clothing woven from two kinds of thread (see Lev. 19:19). Wash-and-wear shirts were, therefore, prohibited because they are made of cotton and a synthetic material. He also claimed that it was wrong to wear at the same time two garments made out of different material. If the shirt was cotton, the pants had to be cotton. (I've often wondered what this man wore for underwear the day he wore his wool suit to church.)

I hear every now and then about Christians who insist that it's wrong for a woman to wear clothing that fits around her legs like a tube (we call them pants). I'll grant you that the Bible says a woman should not wear what pertains to a man (see Deut. 22:5). However, I would like to point out that at the time this was written men and women both wore robes. The difference was not in the garment, but in the way the garment was cut. The same is true of slacks. It's not the trousers, but the way they are cut. You can test this theory for yourself by going to the nearest department store and holding up a pair of men's jeans beside a pair of women's jeans. There *is* a difference.

I have a hard time believing that God intended to make a moral issue out of women wearing men's garments and men wearing women's garments. I think the reason for people to wear garments of their own gender is more practical than it is moral. I'd feel like a jerk wearing my wife's slacks, and I suspect she'd feel about the same in mine.

Making personal preferences a moral issue—Some legalists make a moral issue out of things that are a matter of personal taste or contemporary cultural practice. I can recall, for example, the hand-wringing on the part of some conservative Christians back in the late-1960s and the early-1970s over the long hair and beards that were just coming back into style. Beards were common during the late-1800s, of course, and long hair on men was not all that uncommon. However, both went out of style early in the twentieth century, and by the 1950s our culture had grown so accustomed to men with short hair on top of their heads and none on their chins that we tended to think a man with long hair and a beard was odd. And some conservative Christians were sure that any man who wore long hair and/or a beard must be slipping in his Christian experience. Today precious few would think of judging a man's Christian experience by whether he wore long hair or a beard.

I believe that many of the debates we hear today over music, adornment, the length of a woman's dress (should it be above the knee or below the knee?), modes of Sabbathkeeping, how much sugar to eat, and styles of worship have far more to do with personal preference, cultural conditioning, or both than with biblical morality.

Only one right way—If Scripture is a rule book, then it should be enough to read the rules and apply them. And this leads to another attitude that is characteristic of many legalists: absolute certainty that there is only one correct way to interpret the Scripture regarding standards. And the correct interpretation, of course, is always the legalist's way. Any view that differs from theirs is immediately suspect. Their views seem so obviously correct to them that they wonder how anyone can fail to see it the same way. To put it another way, legalists have a hard time accepting the fact that honest differences of opinion can exist among Christians.

Once they "know" what is right, legalists then proceed to judge the Christian experience of others by this artificial standard. Some legalists will insist that other Christians, and often the church as a whole, adopt their particular point of view.

And this leads us to the third general attitude that has been characteristic of legalism throughout the centuries.

A Desire for Control

A major characteristic of legalism, both ancient and modern, is the desire for control, either of individuals or, in some instances, an entire congregation or even an entire denomination. This, I believe, is where the legalism of the Jewish party most closely resembles that of modern legalists. The Jewish party wanted to control the individual lives of Christians in the early church. In Antioch they tried to control an entire congregation (see Acts 15:1), and as we have seen, in Galatia they tried to control the congregations throughout an entire region.

Legalism is by no means the only way people have used to gain control over other Christians. Some people use money. Others use their position in the community to influence decisions in the church. Still others use anger. A friend of mine who is a pastor in New England told me of a man he knew who used his rage to intimidate an entire congregation into submission. Legalists use their version of morality to control the behavior of other Christians or groups of Christians. Following are some of the characteristics of this form of legalism.

Criticism and intimidation—One of the most common methods used by legalists to control others is criticism and intimidation. Legalists who want to control individuals will assault them verbally over certain things they are doing that they think are wrong. After all, didn't Jesus command us to point out people's sins? (See Matt. 18:15-20.) Women who wear jewelry or pants, Adventists who eat at a restaurant on the Sabbath, people who go to see a motion picture at the theater, will all hear about it from legalists.

Churches can also be the recipients of legalists' efforts to control. Depending on the religious tradition, the use of candles, crosses, Bible versions other than the King James, Christmas trees, and certain styles of music are among the many practices that will bring on the legalists' criticisms. At one time I pastored a congregation that was building a sanctuary, and a few people opposed putting a steeple on the roof because supposedly a pagan culture in the distant past used spires as phallic symbols.

Seldom do legalists succeed at gaining control of a whole congregation or an entire denomination. Their success is in drawing out a group of followers who share their critical spirit and then creating warfare between the two factions. Many congregations, and in some cases entire denominations, have split over matters that at their foundation are a result of legalists attempting to impose their views on the church as a whole.

Every congregation and every denomination will be controlled by someone, of course. In one sense we can say that legalists have as much right to try to control the church as anyone else. The problem with legalists is that they can't accept no for an answer. When they are voted down, they accuse the church of apostasy and keep on criticizing and condemning and trying to draw off a following. This appears to have been the case with the Jewish party. I have taken the position in this book that Paul wrote Galatians after the Jerusalem Council. If that is correct, then even though the Jewish party was thoroughly outvoted at that session, they refused to accept the judgment of the church as a whole and continued to spread their teachings and criticize anyone who refused to go along with them.

A sense of personal responsibility—Legalists tend to feel personally responsible for the morality of others and often for the moral purity of the church as a whole. Didn't God's answer to Cain suggest that he indeed *was* his brother's keeper? (See Gen. 4:1-12.) Didn't God tell Ezekiel to be a watchman on the wall to point out everyone's sin? (See Eze. 33:7-9.) And didn't Jesus tell us to go to a brother who is in sin? (See Matt. 18:15-20.) Legalists use their sense of personal responsibility for the moral behavior of others as justification for pointing out sin as they understand it wherever they see it. Often they will criticize and condemn.

Seldom will legalists admit that they are criticizing and tearing down, however. Legalists who want to control a congregation or a denomination will claim that their motive is to purify the church of sin. In some cases this claim may be sincere. In other cases I am convinced that beneath the expressed desire to help others or to purify the church is a need to gain control that the legalists themselves may not even be aware of.

Playing God—Legalists who try to control the behavior of others with their personal convictions about morality are actually trying to be God to those people. It is appropriate to speak to an individual about a clear case of serious sin. However, lifestyle matters, especially those that are subject to a variety of interpretations, should be left for each individual to decide for himself or herself. We should not keep harassing people over things they are doing that we disagree with. At the very most, such matters deserve one tactful statement and no more, and in most cases it is better to say nothing at all.

There's a general perception among those who try not to be legalistic that legalists are harsh and tactless in their reproach of sin. I've met a few people like that, but most of the legalists I know have tried to be tactful. The issue with legalism is not whether the legalists are tactful or blunt. The issue is their tendency to evaluate (judge) the Christian experience of others by how closely they conform to lifestyle standards as the legalists understand them. Whether they are tactful or blunt, legalists feel that they are personally responsible for the purity of the church and that they must speak out about every departure from biblical standards as they understand them.

Legalism in the family—One of the most tragic situations in which some legalists try to control the behavior of others is in the family. It is the parents' responsibility, of course, to teach their children lifestyle values. The children will never adopt those values if the parents don't teach them. If the parents teach the principles of that lifestyle and not just the behavior—and if they teach their children in a positive, gentle way—the children will likely grow up adopting their parents' values to a large degree. But if every time the parents talk about their values and the lifestyle that goes along with it they pound their views in with quotations from the Bible (and in the case of Adventists, with quotations from Ellen White), they are setting up their children for one of two things. The children will either abandon the parents' values altogether, or they will become legalists themselves.

Parents who hold strong religious convictions tend to feel threatened when their growing children make choices contrary to the parents' convictions of right and wrong. Parents who tend to judge the spiritual experience of others in the church by their adherence to lifestyle standards will feel particularly threatened when their own children violate those standards. They will feel that their children's eternal life is at stake, and they will want to do everything they can to "save" them. I understand the feeling well. I grew up in that kind of environment, not only in my home, but in the entire religious culture of my childhood.

But I've learned that I cannot live my children's spiritual lives for them. My children are adults now, and I have to respect their right to make their own choices, even if I strongly disagree with those choices. I cannot show that respect and at the same time keep on reminding them of my opinion about their choices.

Parents cannot expect to control their children's choices in spiritual matters until the children are 18 and then turn them loose, expecting them to make their own right choices from then on. Much earlier than that, we must accept our children's right to increasingly make moral choices that differ from ours and share our opinion only when asked. We cannot teach our children to make responsible spiritual choices by controlling those choices. The only way to teach them to make their own decisions is to let them make those decisions on their own, free of our continual interference.

That's also how we should relate to one another in the church. The issue is not whether the church has standards in such matters as jewelry, theater attendance, and Sabbathkeeping. The issue is how we will relate to those in the church whose interpretation of those standards differs from ours. We must not try to control each other in these matters.

And that's what legalists have a hard time accepting. Their sense of personal responsibility for the purity of the church causes them to want moral control over others. They do not, and in some cases probably cannot, understand that they are playing God.

Examples of Legalism

One of the best places to get a good look at legalistic thinking in the Adventist Church today is in the letters to the editor columns of the union papers. I'm not condemning union paper editors for publishing these letters. I'm frankly glad they do. It gives me a bit of insight into how others in my church are thinking.

Another excellent way to expose yourself to some of the legalistic thinking in the church is to read the letters that Miriam Wood addresses in her column in the *Adventist Review*. I'd like to quote a few samples from her columns:

"Dear Miriam: I am the father of a 22-year-old son who has his own apartment and is self-supporting. For the past couple of years we have felt him drifting away from the church, and yesterday, Sabbath, we reached a crisis. He skipped Sabbath school, but he came to church service. But he was unhappy when he found that it was Communion day. When the men and women separated for the foot washing, he said, "Dad, would you mind very much if I did not participate today?" I grabbed that big six-footer by the arm, and I told him that he was going to participate and I wouldn't let go of him until we were in the room for the ordinance. He did not say one word through the whole thing. We had invited him to dinner, and when we got home I really set him straight. Perhaps I got a bit carried away because I guess I raised my voice and pounded the table, but doesn't God tell us to see that our children do what is right? My wife is afraid I have alienated him, but I'm sure that I did the right thing. What do you think?"

This is an extreme example of the legalist's great need to control the behavior of others, especially family members. I have no doubt that this father cared about his son. He was desperately anxious that the young man be saved. Unfortunately, he failed to understand that a 22-year-old man has not only the right but also the responsibility to make his own decisions in spiritual matters. The father was playing God to his son. That's one of the great dangers of legalists—to care so much about the salvation of other people that they try to be God to them.

In her reply to this father Miriam Wood said, "I think that you will be fortunate if your son ever enters an Adventist church again."

She's right.

Here's another example:

"Dear Miriam: A group of Sundaykeepers who had no church building have asked to rent our church for several months. I think it would be wrong to allow this since we know that they are keeping the wrong day. Also, the angels and the Holy Spirit will leave the church after the Sabbath hours, so they will be wasting their time anyway."

This person is a legalist. He thinks that anyone who doesn't believe exactly the way he does can't possibly be a Christian and should not be allowed the privileges that we accord to Christians.

Here's one of the most tragic examples of legalism that I've ever run across:

"Dear Miriam: In our small church one of the young girls became pregnant out of wedlock. She did finally marry the baby's father, not an SDA. But they separated after a few weeks. She kept on attending church by herself, and after the baby was born she even asked to have it dedicated. The pastor did this over the objections of some of the members. It seems to some of us that she ought to be ashamed even to show her face, and that having the baby publicly dedicated shamed the entire church. What do you think?"

Here is Miriam's answer:

"Perhaps you would prefer that she be forced to wear a scarlet letter A on her clothing so that she would be sure to suffer all the days of her life for her mistake. May I ask you a question? What sin has the baby committed? I can certainly understand your concern for the good name of the church, but that can never supersede the need to extend unqualified love in such cases."

God tells us to love sinners, and it doesn't make any difference what the sin is. The woman who said, "This girl who had a baby out of wedlock shamed the church; she should have been thrown out of the church," was a modern-day Pharisee. The Pharisees, you will recall, are the ones who said to Jesus' disciples, "Why does your Master associate with sinners?" (See Luke 15:2.) That's legalism.

Here's another letter.

"Dear Miriam: I'm writing to you with a very heavy heart. But I want you to know that I love the Adventist Church and I will never leave it, even though I feel so rejected and lonely that at times I can hardly endure it. I'm a lifelong SDA, but my husband is not. He is a wonderful man, moral, upright in every way, and has always allowed me to practice my religion freely. He has sent our three children through our schools and paid all their bills cheerfully. But the members in our small rural church will not associate with us because, as one lady told me, 'First Corinthians 5:11 means that we must stay away from people who do not belong to our church and keep all of God's laws and Ellen White's teachings.'

"Once a picnic was planned by the church for a Sabbath afternoon in the park, and I was so happy because I thought that the children and I could go. But one of the members said, 'This is not for divided families, and you wouldn't enjoy it.' The children cried, they were so disappointed.

"In summer, Sabbath afternoons have always seemed so long because no one ever comes to see us, and we feel unwelcome if we call on others. We have tried so hard to be friendly, but nothing happens. When my mother died, though she was not an Adventist, she had requested that our pastor conduct her funeral, which he did. But none of the church members ever came back to our house.

"If you publish this letter, I pray that perhaps others may see the needs some of us have in a divided home and how much simple friendship would mean."

Each of these letters is an example of cold, blatant legalism. Uncaring, unloving, unchristian legalism. I hate to say it, but every one of those letters was written by a Seventh-day Adventist, and they reflect the attitude of all too many of us. It's the same attitude Paul condemned in Galatians when he said, "You foolish Galatians! Who has bewitched you!" It's the same attitude he didn't want his Gentile brothers and sisters in Galatia going back to. It's the same kind of person Paul told the Galatians to get rid of. The Gentiles were troubled by circumcision and feast days—ceremonial legalism—in their day. We are troubled by lifestyle legalism in our day.

In chapter 16 we will discuss the consequences of this kind of thinking. However, before we move on to the next chapter I need to keep my promise and discuss the quiz you took at the beginning of this chapter. Count the number of yes answers you gave on the quiz and then circle that number on the line below:

```
1      2      3      4      5      6      7      8      9    10
|      |      |      |      |      |      |      |      |     |
|                                                           |
|_____|
```

The quiz and the "scoring diagram" are obviously not scientific. I thought up the whole thing, both the questions and the diagram, in about an hour. Yet despite the simplicity of the quiz, I believe there is an element of truth about ourselves that each of us can discover by answering those questions honestly and by circling our score on the diagram. I would like to suggest that the closer your number is to 10, the more seriously you need to ask yourself, "Am I a legalist?"

You may think this is a trivial question. It's not. The closer you scored to 10, the more seriously you need to ask yourself whether your attitude—your desire for purity in the church—may actually be creating a coldness that is driving people away. This is especially true if by the time you finished the quiz you felt angry, because the mere fact that I would ask such questions suggests that I am a liberal.

Unfortunately, most legalists do not realize that they are legalists. It is extremely difficult for legalists to recognize the damage their attitudes are doing in the lives of other people. If you scored anywhere near 10—and certainly if you scored a 9 or a 10, I urge you to ask God to help you understand yourself and your attitudes. Ask Him to show you what your words and actions are doing to others. Ask Him to change your heart and make you a kind, loving Christian who can win people to Jesus instead of driving them to Him—or away from Him.

The Consequences of Legalism
Galatians 5:1-15

A man in a church that I used to attend told me one day that he was getting exasperated by a certain older woman in the church who kept reproving him and his wife for the clothes they wore, the food they ate, the entertainment they chose, the way they kept the Sabbath, the programs they watched on TV, ad nauseam. "She's a sincere little old woman," he said, "and I know she means well. But frankly, I'm becoming weary of it."

"Tell her it's none of her business," I said.

"That's hard to do," he replied. "She's a friend of the family, and she comes over to our home just about every day."

I dropped the matter, since it was none of *my* business how he handled his friend. However, his story does illustrate the lesson that Paul shared with us in the first half of Galatians 5. Paul said: "It is for freedom that Christ has set us free. Stand firm, then, and do not let yourselves be burdened again by a yoke of slavery. Mark my words! I, Paul, tell you that if you let yourselves be circumcised, Christ will be of no value to you at all. Again I declare to every man who lets himself be circumcised that he is obligated to obey the whole law" (verses 1-3).

Paul said it was for freedom that Christ set us free. What does it mean to be free?

For one thing, it means to be free of the notion that we are responsible for everyone else's behavior in the church, or even in our own family. It also means to be free of people who think they are responsible for our behavior. And of course, it means to be free of the mistaken idea that our salvation somehow depends on keeping all the standards.

I'm not trying to do away with standards. I'm simply trying to put them in their place. Standards help us lead exemplary lives, and every Christian ought to strive for that. But standards do not save us. Keeping them does not save us. Only Jesus and faith in Him can do that. Freedom in Christ sets us free of the notion that keeping the standards saves us.

Next Paul said: "Stand firm, then, and do not let yourselves be burdened again by a yoke of slavery." Notice that Paul did not say the Galatian Christians were imposing a yoke of bondage on themselves. This burden was being imposed on them by someone else. And that someone else was, of course, the Jewish party.

Christian freedom means, among other things, that we are responsible to God for our behavior and that we should not allow others to dictate to us their understanding of how we ought to live. My friend, who was weary of the controlling influence of the family friend, did not know how to do that. However, Paul's advice to this man and his wife is clear: Stand firm; do not allow yourselves to be burdened by a yoke of slavery. Do not allow others, regardless of their professed sincerity, to pressure you into conformance to their lifestyle. Nor should you allow others to harass you about it.

Standards of Christian behavior are a yoke of slavery when we impose them on ourselves and use them as a measure of our spiritual experience and our standing with God. They are doubly a yoke of slavery when we allow others to impose their understanding of standards on us and judge the quality of our Christian experience by their ideas of right and wrong. There are two ways we can allow others to do this to us. One is by yielding to their moral pressure, conforming our behavior to their convictions even though our convictions don't demand it. The other way is to live according to our convictions, but continually feel guilty because others keep insisting we're wrong. Either way, we are allowing someone else to impose a yoke of slavery on us.

The only way I know to handle this problem is to follow Paul's advice: Stand firm. Don't allow it. This means doing what my friend was unwilling to do—saying to the persecutor (for that's what he or she is), "I am responsible to God for my behavior, not to you, and our friendship can continue only if you stop getting after me for the things I do that you disapprove of." You don't have to speak in anger, but you do need to be firm. You are not telling this person that you will never talk to him or her again, or associate with him or her in church, but only that the present level of friendship cannot continue if the efforts to control your life keep up. This is what it means to "get rid of the slave woman and her son" (Gal. 4:30).

The consequences of not taking this firm stand can be serious. Paul said, "Mark my words! I, Paul, tell you that if you let yourselves be circumcised, Christ will be of no value to you at all." That's strong language!

Paul did not say to the Galatian Christians, "Don't circumcise your-selves." He said, "Do not let yourselves *be* circumcised" by others. Once again he called attention to the Jewish party's efforts to impose its value system onto the Galatian Christians, and he said, "Don't allow that."

"But no one is pressuring Christians today to be circumcised," you say. "Paul's advice has nothing to do with today's standards of behavior."

It's true that the particular behavior in Paul's day was different from what it is today. But as I pointed out in the previous chapter, the issue with Galatian legalism was control. When that becomes the issue with legalism today, it's just as wrong as it was then either to impose our view of morality onto others or to allow them to impose their convictions on us. Whether the convictions are about circumcision, diet, entertainment, Sabbathkeeping, or dress, the issue is the same. Others have their lives to live before God, and you and I have ours. We are each responsible to God and to no one else for the way we live. Anytime we allow someone else to occupy that place in our lives, Christ has become of no value to us.

This does not mean that the church should have nothing to say about the lives of its members. Paul instructed the Corinthian believers to disfellowship a man who was carrying on a sexual relationship with his father's wife (probably his stepmother). Sexual immorality, theft, blasphemy, and murder are among the sins that a church can very properly discipline its members for. Seventh-day Adventists include the use of alcohol, tobacco, and street drugs among those behaviors for which members can be disciplined.

Yet even here the issue should not be to control the lives of other people. Anyone should be free to drink, smoke, and behave sexually the way he or she wants to, so long as that behavior conforms to the law of the land. The church is simply saying that a person cannot do these things and expect to retain membership in the church. Any organization has a right to state the conditions for becoming and remaining a member of its group, and the church is no exception.

The difference with respect to lifestyle issues is the degree of "sinfulness" involved and the possibility for differences of opinion that can exist among converted people. The church must discipline serious sins such as adultery, but we should respect differences of opinion about less important matters, especially where there are no clear guidelines and it's a matter of personal judgment what is right and what is wrong.

For example, one Christian woman can in good conscience wear a shorter dress, while another woman feels strongly that her dress should be longer. One person enjoys one style of music, and someone else prefers another. One person can watch a TV program that his or her Christian friend would find offensive.

The issue is not whether one person is right and the other wrong. I see people every now and then doing things that my conscience would not allow me to do. The issue is whether the people I see doing things that to me would be wrong have a right to live in harmony with their consciences, free of pressure from me and free of my gossip about their behavior.

Some people seem to be emotionally and intellectually incapable of acknowledging that such differences of opinion can be tolerated and still have a "good" church. As they see it, every issue is either black or white, and so clearly black or white that every Christian ought to be able to agree on which is which. Of course, as I pointed out in the previous chapter, these people are always sure that their view is the only right view, and anyone who thinks otherwise is on the wrong side. They cannot allow for a variety of views—what we sometimes call pluralism. Such people are among the worst legalists in the church. They can split a church down the middle. They can drive scores of weaker Christians out of the church. And through it all they can piously congratulate themselves for upholding the standards.

I would like to discuss an issue that is a growing point of contention in the Adventist Church: jewelry. For the first 40 years of my life I could tell the difference between the women in church who were Adventists and those who were not. The Adventist women never wore jewelry. When I welcomed a guest to church who was wearing earrings, necklaces, or bracelets, I knew I was welcoming a person who was not an Adventist.

However, during the seventies, and increasingly during the eighties, Adventist women began wearing jewelry, especially small earrings and to a lesser extent necklaces. I still remember several years ago making a conscious decision not to judge these women for their choice of adornment. This was between them and God, not them and me. It's entirely possible that in some cases these women's relationship with God was less than ideal. I let that be their business. To this day I refuse to think less of such people for their choice. I refuse to speak to them about their choice. And I refuse to criticize their choice in the presence of others.

Now let's look at the consequences of legalism. Paul said: "You who are trying to be justified by law have been alienated from Christ; you have fallen away from grace. But by faith we eagerly await through the Spirit the righteousness for which we hope. For in Christ Jesus neither circumcision nor uncircumcision has any value. The only thing that counts is faith expressing itself through love" (Gal. 5:4-6).

In this passage Paul made some pointed remarks about people who try to be justified by law. Some Christians fail to apply this advice to themselves because they claim to believe in righteousness by faith. But their insistence on judging people's spirituality by their conformance to behavioral standards is clear evidence that law is more important to them than grace. Paul said two things about people who try to be justified by law: (1) they "have been alienated from Christ," and (2) they "have fallen away from grace."

To be alienated from Christ means to have no relationship with Him. If a relationship with Jesus is what saves, then to be alienated from Christ means to have no relationship with Him, and the consequence of that is to lose eternal life.

Paul went a step further and said: "You who are trying to be justified by law . . . have fallen away from grace." To fall from grace means to fall from the saved condition that comes when one is under grace. It means to be lost.

The consequences of legalism are serious!

But enough of legalism for the moment. What is the true Christian like? Paul said: "By faith we eagerly await through the Spirit the righteousness for which we hope." The righteousness "for which we hope" is in contrast to the righteousness according to law, taught by the Jewish party.

One question we can raise here is this: When Paul spoke of "the righteousness for which we hope," did he have in mind the righteousness of Christ that substitutes for our sinful behavior and thus saves us, which is justification? Or did he have in mind the righteous behavior of the Christian who has been transformed on the inside, which we commonly call sanctification?

A careful look at the text suggests to me that Paul had in mind sanctification. In the first place, justification, which gives us our legal standing with God, is not something for which the Christian hopes. To hope means to anticipate something in the future. But justification comes instantly, the moment we confess our sins and put our faith in Christ. Justification provides our assurance of salvation, and we don't have to hope for that. We can *know* that we have it *now* (see 1 John 5:12, 13).

Sanctification, on the other hand, comes more gradually. It can truly be said that we hope for a change in our behavior through transformation of heart.

In Galatians 5:6 Paul said: "For in Christ Jesus neither circumcision nor uncircumcision has any value. The only thing that counts is faith expressing itself through love." Many legalists find it difficult to express love for those who violate their standards of behavior. Do you remember the examples of legalism that I mentioned in the previous chapter? One characteristic that was common to all four of them was the inability of those who felt offended to show love toward those whom they perceived to be sinners. Legalists will say, "Your presence is damaging the morals of the church." True Christians will say, "I'm so glad to see you in church today." They'll put their arms around the sinner and say, "I care about you." True Christians don't frown at sinners. They smile at them.

Perhaps you've begun to recognize yourself in the descriptions I've given of legalism in this chapter and in previous chapters. If you're a legalist, I hope you have recognized yourself. And I say that kindly, because I have good news for you. God can forgive legalism just as He can forgive any other sin. More than that, He can help you overcome your legalism. It *is* possible to escape from legalism. It's probably one of the most difficult sins to escape from because it's so hard to recognize in ourselves. But don't be discouraged by the fact that it's *difficult*. What counts is that it's *possible*. We'll discuss this in much greater detail in the next chapter.

Let's talk about Galatians 5:7-12: "You were running a good race. Who cut in on you and kept you from obeying the truth? That kind of persuasion does not come from the one who calls you. 'A little yeast works through the whole batch of dough.' I am confident in the Lord that you will take no other view. The one who is throwing you into confusion will pay the penalty, whoever he may be. Brothers, if I am still preaching circumcision, why am I still being persecuted? In that case the offense of the cross has been abolished. As for those agitators, I wish they would go the whole way and emasculate themselves!"

Paul spoke quite specifically about the troublemakers in Galatia. He didn't name any names, but there can be no doubt that he was talking about particular people. He said, "You were running a good race. Who cut in on you?" Of course, the Galatian Christians knew who had cut in on them. They knew exactly who the members of the Jewish party were, and they knew who these people's sympathizers were in the Galatian congregations.

In verse 10 Paul said, "The one who is throwing you into confusion will pay the penalty, whoever he may be." Notice that Paul used the singular in referring to the Jewish party. He probably had a specific person in mind. A group of people had infiltrated the Galatian churches and one of them was no doubt the leader, and that's why Paul spoke of "the *one* who is throwing you into confusion." Paul could have given an actual name. He probably knew the name, but he tactfully left that out of a letter intended for public reading in the church. That's an example of handling legalists in the church firmly but also kindly.

Finally Paul said—and this is a good clue that more than one representative of the Jewish party had come to Galatia—"As for these agitators, I wish they would go the whole way and emasculate themselves!" Emasculate as used here means to castrate. Paul really got worked up! He actually said, "I wish these agitators would go the whole way and castrate themselves."

Paul said something in verse 9 that I find extremely significant: "A little yeast works through the whole batch of dough." Paul meant that if it was allowed to go unchecked, the legalistic spirit of the Jewish party would eventually poison the entire Christian body in Galatia.

The same is true today. Legalism that is not checked will spread and grow. And there is a good reason: at first glance it seems so reasonable. We humans cannot see what people's hearts are like, but we can see what their behavior is like. So we set up standards by which to measure behavior, and then we judge that behavior. Before long the judgmental spirit of one person, which seems so reasonable because it's visible and measurable, has spread throughout the whole church. Like a spoonful of yeast, it has worked through the whole batch of dough. Like a tiny malignant cancer, it has infected the whole body.

The solution to this problem is found, I believe, in 1 Corinthians 4:5: "Therefore judge nothing before the appointed time; wait till the Lord comes. He will bring to light what is hidden in darkness and will expose the motives of men's hearts."

The reason God tells us not to judge each other in this world is not a lack of intelligence on our part. It's a lack of information. We cannot read the heart. Persons whom we judge to be sinners by outward observation may actually have a close relationship with Jesus on the inside. On the other hand, persons whose behavior appears to us to be most exemplary may, in fact, be indulging in the grossest sin in their hearts and private lives.

We are intelligent enough to judge each other now. And one of these days, beginning with the second coming of Christ, God will supply us with all the data for doing that. At that time "he will bring to light what is hidden in darkness and will expose the motives of men's hearts." Then we will have a perfect right to evaluate the Christian experience of others, especially those who have not joined us in God's kingdom. Then we will understand, as God and the angels do now, why some people who appear so exemplary in this life will be lost in the next. We will also understand why some whom we thought would never make it to God's kingdom are there.

Legalism is actually the effort to use our intelligence, which is adequate, to judge others based on data that is inadequate. Unfortunately, because legalism is so visible and measurable, it seems adequate; it seems reasonable and right. And that's why it can spread so rapidly throughout an entire congregation.

It takes special spiritual discernment on the part of the leaders of a congregation to prevent this spirit from taking control of an entire church.

I like what Paul said at the beginning of Galatians 5:10: "I am confident in the Lord that you will take no other view." Paul expressed confidence in the Galatian Christians. This is one of the things that legalists find so hard to do. They can't trust others to make right judgments. That's why they try so hard to impose their own judgment on them. They are afraid that others will make mistakes. In their "great love" and "deep concern" for others, they want to help them find eternal life. Legalists would rather wring their hands about sin in the church than believe that sinners in their own relationship with God can conquer those sins.

Paul was not that way. He expressed full confidence that the Galatian Christians would overcome this temptation to legalism, that they would put it behind them and grow in their Christian experience. I believe his confidence was especially strong that the leaders in the Galatian congregations would prevent the legalism of the Jewish party from taking control of their churches. He trusted these leaders to "get rid of the slave woman and her son" (Gal. 4:30).

Let's talk briefly about Galatians 5:13-15: "You, my brothers, were called to be free. But do not use your freedom to indulge the sinful nature; rather, serve one another in love. The entire law is summed up in a single command: 'Love your neighbor as yourself.' If you keep on biting and devouring each other, watch out or you will be destroyed by each other."

On one point I have to agree with the legalists. High standards of Christian deportment are important. Paul emphasized that when he said, "You, my brothers, were called to be free. But *do not use your freedom to indulge the sinful nature.*" Christian standards are a way that we define the kind of behavior that is acceptable and the kind of behavior that is not acceptable under the law of love for others. The problem is that legalists get the standard ahead of the love. To them it's most important that a person be in harmony with the law of love, and they fail to understand how unloving they are in their efforts to "help" others.

Paul was not interested in letting down the standards of the church or the standards of the Bible. Christians must not indulge the sinful nature, and therefore, Christians will not behave in ways that are obviously an expression of the sinful nature. But the motive behind those high standards must be love for others, and not a keeping of the law for its own sake. Those who insist on high standards without love and who try to control others are indulging their own version of the sinful nature.

I would like to conclude this chapter with verse 15: "If you keep on biting and devouring each other, watch out or you will be destroyed by each other."

Rarely will the legalistic attitudes of a few people spread to an entire congregation. What is much more likely to occur is a division in the church between those who adopt the legalists' narrow views and those who do not. Unfortunately, legalists with a strong need to control are difficult to deal with because they refuse to stop their criticism. In due time this leads to something that is almost as bad as the entire congregation becoming legalistic—warfare in the church.

And that is most likely what happened in Galatia. The Jewish party's insistence on Gentile observance of circumcision and other Jewish ceremonial laws had divided the Galatian Christians into two camps. By the time Paul wrote Galatians, the division had intensified to a war of words— anger, accusations, charges, and countercharges. The division may have occurred largely along ethnic lines, Jewish Christians siding with the Jewish party, and Gentile Christians siding with Paul.

When we think of legalism as an issue of control, then it is inevitable that this division should have occurred in the Galatian congregations. Such divisions are bound to occur in any congregation where one group tries to control another. And sooner or later this problem will lead to hurt feelings, shattered relationships, and ruined lives. Thousands of young people have given up their relationship to the church, and some have abandoned their relationship with God, as well, because of the efforts of legalists in the church to control them. Jesus said it would be better for such people to be cast into the sea with a millstone hung around their neck (see Luke 17:1, 2). No wonder Paul warned the Galatian Christians, "If you keep on biting and devouring each other, watch out or you will be destroyed by each other"!

That's why it's so important that we have a correct understanding of standards and how to relate to standards in our relationships with one another. That's why it's so important that we learn to be loving, understanding, and kind to those who do not see things exactly as we do, or who have not progressed as far in their Christian experience as we have.

I am reminded of a statement by G. R. Beasley-Murray: "The road to the cross has always been easier for the publican than for the Pharisee."*

Let us make our journey to the cross as easy as possible! Let us pray that God will help us understand the legalism in our own hearts. Let us ask Him to help us understand what it really means to be free in Jesus.

---

*The New Century Bible Commentary: Revelation (London: Marshall, Morgan, and Scott, 1974), p. 105.

CHAPTER 17

Gaining the Victory Over Legalism
Galatians 5:16-26

Several summers ago my wife and I attended a seminar on Seventh-day Adventist history at Andrews University. One of the participants in the seminar was a gentleman whom I would judge to have been about 75 years old at the time.

One day my wife and I ate our noon meal in the cafeteria with this man, and as the conversation progressed, he said, "I used to be a died-in-the-wool legalist. I'm sure I was most unpleasant to be around. I must have made life miserable for my poor wife. But about three years ago the minister at my church preached a series on righteousness by faith, and I began to see what I was really like. I am thankful that God has changed my life. He's transformed my heart, and I'm no longer a legalist."

As my wife and I talked to this man we realized that he indeed *had* been a legalist and that he no longer *was* a legalist. Later in our room we said, "Praise God. If it can happen to a 75-year-old man, it can happen to anybody!" Age makes no difference when it comes to God transforming hearts.

Yes, victory over legalism is possible. And that is the theme of the last half of Galatians 5. The easiest way to understand this passage, I believe, will be to look at it first as a whole, then to discuss the details. That way we can move among the verses as we need to instead of examining them a verse at a time or a section at a time. That will be a much better way to proceed in this particular case. Here are verses 16, 17: "So I say, live by the Spirit, and you will not gratify the desires of the sinful nature.[1] For the sinful nature desires what is contrary to the Spirit, and the Spirit what is contrary to the sinful nature."

The main point we need to notice in these verses is the conflict between the sinful nature and the Spirit. In verses 19-23 Paul elaborated on each of these. Here is what he said about the sinful nature: "The acts of the sinful nature are obvious: sexual immorality, impurity and debauchery; idolatry and witchcraft; hatred, discord, jealousy, fits of rage, selfish ambition, dissensions, factions and envy; drunkenness, orgies, and the like. I warn you, as I did before, that those who live like this will not inherit the kingdom of God" (verses 19-21).

Paul also elaborated on the Spirit and His influence in the life of the Christian: "But the fruit of the Spirit is love, joy, peace, patience, kindness, goodness, faithfulness, gentleness and self-control. Against such things there is no law" (verses 22, 23).

Paul then concluded the chapter with a brief comment about how Christians can live by the Spirit instead of by the sinful nature: "Those who belong to Christ Jesus have crucified the sinful nature with its passions and desires. Since we live by the Spirit, let us keep in step with the Spirit. Let us not become conceited, provoking and envying each other" (verses 24-26).

The question we need to ask is Why did Paul go to such great lengths, near the conclusion of his response to the Jewish party, to elaborate on the sinful nature and life in the Spirit? The answer is quite simple: legalism destroys true spirituality and ultimately leads legalists down the very path they are so anxious to avoid—living a life of sin that is in harmony with the sinful nature. And they do it under the delusion that they are progressing toward holiness!

I have mentioned before in this book that the members of the Jewish party who came to Galatia were utterly sincere in their desire to help the Galatian Christians experience salvation. I can see them now, kneeling in the home of one of their faithful followers, pleading with God to "open the way for Your truth to advance throughout Galatia." I've prayed many prayers like that myself. How could anyone that sincere be so wrong?

Unfortunately, I can also visualize their determination to break Paul's influence in the Galatian churches. I can hear their criticism of his theology, their effort to discredit him by questioning the genuineness of his apostleship. Everything was said with the appropriate religious words, to be sure. But Paul recognized the motive behind their pious language.

Let's go back to the beginning of the passage we are considering in this chapter. In fact, we actually need to start with Galatians 5:15, which we discussed at the conclusion of the previous chapter. Here is that verse along with verses 16 and 17: "If you keep on biting and devouring each other, watch out or you will be destroyed by each other. So I say, live by the Spirit, and you will not gratify the desires of the sinful nature. For the sinful nature desires what is contrary to the Spirit, and the Spirit what is contrary to the sinful nature. They are in conflict with each other, so that you do not do what you want."

The "biting and devouring" that Paul spoke about in verse 15 resulted from the efforts of members of the Jewish party to force their views onto the Galatian congregations. Those in the Galatian congregations who opposed them probably did not have enough maturity to handle the problem without getting upset themselves, and that's why quarrelling and criticizing broke out in the various congregations.

With this in mind, let's read verse 16: "Live by the Spirit," Paul said, "and you will not gratify the desires of the sinful nature."

Two things are significant about this verse. First is the fact that the backbiting and criticism that resulted from the legalism of the Jewish party was a manifestation of the sinful nature, and that was true of both sides in the argument. The Jewish party's criticism of Paul and their effort to force the Gentiles into compliance with Old Testament ceremonial law may have been the source of the conflict, but both sides were displaying their sinful nature.

I find it most significant that legalism is a demonstration of the very sinful nature that legalists are so eager to condemn in others. That's why it is such a difficult sin to recognize in ourselves. Those of us who are legalists feel so good that we aren't "bad" that it never occurs to us that our very condemnation may be just as evil as the sins we oppose in others.

However—and this brings us to the second important thought in verse 16—in the same breath he used to point out the problem, Paul also pointed out the solution: *Live by the Spirit,* he said, "and you will not gratify the desires of the sinful nature." Victory over any form of legalism comes as we learn how to live by the Spirit.

If legalism arises out of the sinful nature, then the key to victory over legalism is learning to live in the Spirit. I would like to discuss life in the Spirit with you in the context of the process we go through to gain the victory over sin. We will begin with the first step that Christians must take to conquer sin in their lives and proceed to the last. I should explain first, though, that we are going to take a detour from Galatians for a few minutes, because in Galatians Paul only discussed the first and the last of the steps that I want to review with you. The other steps are totally biblical. It's just that Paul didn't mention them here.

The first step in gaining the victory over any sin is to recognize that it is a sin and that we are guilty of it. We call this *conviction*. Conviction is also the Christian's first step toward a life in the Spirit, because it is the Holy Spirit that convicts of sin. "When he [the Holy Spirit] comes," Jesus said, "he will *convict* the world of . . . sin" (John 16:8).

One of the most important ways that the Holy Spirit convicts us of sin is through the Bible. And since Paul was a Bible writer, the Spirit could use his letter to the Galatian Christians to convict them of sin.

Actually, in the life of genuine Christians, conviction of sin never stops. Christians are always open to the Spirit showing another area of their lives that needs to be surrendered to Jesus Christ, forgiven, and cleansed by His blood. Conviction is the first step in the process of sinners becoming Christians, because it begins even before they are Christians. Jesus said that none of us would come to Him in the first place if He didn't draw us (see John 6:44), though it is the Holy Spirit who actually works on our minds and hearts to draw us to Jesus.

Not only did God use Paul's letter to the Galatians to convict them of the sin of legalism that the Jewish party was trying to push onto them; I think God used that letter to try to convict the Jewish party themselves of the true nature of their attitudes and behavior. We do not know, of course, whether any members of the Jewish party recognized the truth of Paul's statements, but I think a large number of the Galatian Christians, including Jewish Christians in Galatia, must have yielded to the Holy Spirit's conviction and abandoned their legalism. I certainly hope so.

Legalism is not the temptation of just a few. It is a temptation to every one of us. I believe there is something of the legalist in every Christian. We all have to resist the idea that we can do something to merit salvation. And I suspect that each of us is tempted from time to time to push our views of morality onto others. When we understand what Paul said to the Galatians, God can use this letter to convict every one of us of the legalism in ourselves.

Unfortunately, as I pointed out earlier, legalists tend to be the last to recognize their own legalism or to understand that it is a sin. Does that mean there is no hope for legalists?

Absolutely not—or, as Paul would say, "God forbid" (Gal. 3:21, KJV). I have good news for you. There *is* hope for the legalist. And since there is a little bit of the legalist in all of us, what I say next applies to everyone reading this book, myself included.

Let's begin with the root of the problem: none of us enjoys admitting that we are wrong. We know theoretically that we're sinners, and in a general sense we don't mind admitting that. In fact, it puts us in pretty good company, since everyone is a sinner. But we hate getting too specific about our sins. "Yes, Lord, I'm a sinner—but surely You aren't talking about that . . . or that . . . or that!" Believe me, legalists aren't alone in denying specific sins! We all do it all the time.

But whose opinion counts most when it comes to telling the truth about whether this or that specific behavior or character trait is sinful—God's or yours and mine? I think we would all agree that God's opinion is the *only* one that counts. So we really have no business telling God anything about our sins. If we are serious about salvation, our main task is not to tell Him what we think about our lives but to listen to what He thinks about our lives.

Since legalism is an almost universal human trait, why shouldn't each of us begin with the assumption that we have almost certainly been tempted to be legalistic, and in some ways it's likely we *are* legalists, even if it is just a tiny bit. Furthermore, if we have even the slightest tendency toward legalism, God knows it. In fact, the smaller our tendency is in that direction, the less likely it is that we will be aware of it, which means He is the *only* one who knows it.

With these thoughts in mind, here's what I've done, and what I suggest you do. Ask God to show you any tendency that you may have toward legalism. In other words, invite Him to convict you. Say "God, show me if You see any way in which I'm a legalist."

If you really don't want to say that prayer, let me share a couple of thoughts with you. The first one is a question I raised earlier: Whose opinion counts most anyway—yours or God's? Are you afraid of what He might tell you? That's dangerous ground for any Christian to tread on!

The second point is this: that prayer—"God, show me if You see any way in which I'm a legalist"—is not going to jump out and bite you. Believe me, it's a perfectly safe prayer. It won't give you cancer. It won't even give you a stomachache. So even if you feel certain you aren't a legalist, don't be afraid of that prayer. In fact, the more certain you are that you're *not* a legalist, the less you have to fear about that prayer. Because if you're as right as you believe you are, then God agrees with you and isn't about to convict you of something you aren't guilty of. On the other hand, I think you'll agree that if, in spite of your certainty to the contrary, you really *are* a legalist in certain ways, then you of all people *need* to know it and should *want* to know it.

So go ahead and say that prayer: "God, show me if You see any way in which I'm a legalist."

Once you've said it, what can you expect to happen?

Probably nothing at first. I doubt that God will flash any words in the sky. You aren't likely to see a vision or hear voices coming from outer space. God's conviction of your legalism, if He has any such conviction for you, will almost certainly come much more subtly than that. Just keep saying that prayer once a day for at least a month. If you really are a legalist in some way, big or small, God will begin to make that clear to you through the events in your everyday life. That's His usual way of working.

Conviction is the first step as sinners move toward salvation. The second step is repentance. Conviction is the Holy Spirit telling you what's wrong with your life. Repentance is you admitting that He's right. In conviction, you and I are largely passive. The Holy Spirit takes the initiative to put thoughts into our minds, and He doesn't even ask for our permission. But in repentance we choose to accept what He tells us about our sins. God will not force us to repent. However, nobody would ever repent on his or her own. Again, He *draws* us to repentance. Even though He won't force us to accept His verdict about our sins, He gives us the power to make that choice. It's like a baby holding his hand up toward the cookie jar on the counter and the mother picking him up so he can reach inside and take a cookie.

Actually, any time we say that *God* does something for us in our minds, such as convicting us or helping us to repent, it's the *Holy Spirit* who actually does it. The Holy Spirit is the member of the Trinity who dwells in us (see John 14:17). Thus, repentance is also a part of what Paul meant in Galatians when he spoke about "life in the Spirit."

Let's say that at least once a day and sometimes two or three times a day, you've been saying that prayer I suggested: "God, show me if You see any way in which I'm a legalist." One day about a week later you're talking to a friend on the phone, when suddenly the thought crosses your mind that some words you just spoke are similar to something you read a chapter or two back in this book. A few days later in church you hear someone else say the same kind of thing, and again the thought crosses your mind that you read about that in this book. The same thing happens two or three times during the following week, and by the next Sabbath you're beginning to wonder if that's the Holy Spirit trying to tell you something.

The Lord has a thousand ways to bring the conviction to your mind that you're a legalist. The scenario I just gave you is an example of how He might do it. He has lots of other ways. Within a week after you start asking Him to show you if you're a legalist, He might be so direct as to have someone say flat out to your face, "You're a legalist." Now, that would be some answer to your prayer!

Whatever way the Lord chooses to bring the thought to your mind that you might be a legalist, your next step, as I pointed out earlier, needs to be repentance. Unfortunately, if you're like most of us sinners, you won't feel like repenting just because the Lord showed you that you need to. So how can you repent when you don't want to?

I can tell you one way that won't work: forcing yourself. You can choose to repent, just as a baby can choose to get a cookie out of the jar. But you can't *actually* repent until the Holy Spirit "picks you up" and helps you do it. So I suggest that you say two more prayers. First, say, "Lord, if that's You talking, and if You really *are* trying to tell me I'm a legalist on this point, then keep bringing this thought back to me." Your second prayer is really just an addition to the first one: "And Lord, if that really is You talking, then help me *want* to accept what You're telling me, even though right now I don't feel like accepting it." That's asking the Lord to lift you up so you can put your hand in the cookie jar. It's asking Him to help you repent.

You really don't have a thing to lose by saying these prayers. The Lord isn't going to tell you that you're a legalist if you aren't one. On the other hand, if you are a legalist, then you want to know that so you can deal with it. Either way *you win!*

Life in the Spirit isn't so bad after all, is it? Actually, it's just cooperating with what we've known all along that God wants to do for us and in us.

If the Lord shows you that you've been a legalist in what seems to be some small way, think of it as a clue that there may be other ways you still have no idea about. Keep saying those prayers. God *will* keep answering them!

If you discover that you have been a harsh legalist for many years, the sudden realization that you've hurt many, many people during your lifetime could leave you feeling quite overwhelmed. Here is where the third step is absolutely essential: confession and forgiveness. I put these two to-gether because God does. "If we confess our sins," the Bible says, "he is faithful and just to forgive us our sins, and to cleanse us from all unrigh-teousness" (1 John 1:9, KJV).

Victory over *any* sin requires confession. Alcoholics who conquer their habit through Alcoholics Anonymous have learned that. Only in the past 50 years has the world known of a way that alcoholics could be certain of controlling their habit. Prior to that, few people actually overcame alco-holism. I am convinced that AA succeeds because it is such a deeply spiri-tual method for dealing with the problem. And I find it extremely significant that several of the 12 steps of AA have to do with acknowledg-ing and confessing sin—in the case of AA, the sin of alcoholism. Here are the steps I have in mind:

Step 4: "Made a searching and fearless moral inventory of ourselves."

Step 5: "Admitted to God, to ourselves, and to another human being the exact nature of our wrongs."

Step 8: "Made a list of all persons we had harmed, and became willing to make amends to them all."

Step 9: "Made direct amends to such people wherever possible, except when to do so would injure them or others."

The 12 steps of AA work with people of all religious faiths who really try them. They work with people who have no particular religious faith. They even work with people who don't believe in God! AA has demon-strated this time and time again.

The question is Why?

I believe the answer is that God made the human mind to work this way. Confession is a profoundly spiritual activity. Admitting our faults to ourselves and confessing them to those we have harmed is His way for anyone to conquer a bad habit. That's why He tells us about it in Scripture.

If you are serious about overcoming the legalism God shows you, then it is essential that you make amends to those who have been harmed by your attitudes and your words. This can be extremely difficult. In fact, some people have found it impossible. But the good news is that it doesn't have to be. There's another prayer you can say to deal with the pain and the difficulty of confession: "God, help me *want* to confess this sin."

Once you have confessed, then you have a perfect right to claim God's forgiveness fully and completely. "*If* we confess," the Bible says—and when you do confess, you've met that condition—"he is faithful and just to forgive."

God's forgiveness has two aspects. First, it is a legal transaction that happens on His books of record in heaven. He writes "forgiven" across that sin. In fact, the Bible says that He blots it out (see Isa. 44:22)! He treats you as though you'd never done it.

The second aspect of forgiveness happens in your mind and heart. You have a sense of peace, because you know that God accepts you just as you are. "Therefore, since we have been justified through faith," Paul said, "we have peace with God through our Lord Jesus Christ" (Rom. 5:1). Some people find that this peace does not come immediately after they confess a sin. If that happens to you, ask God to bring it to you. In His own time and way, He will. I think it's also important to remember that you may continue to feel sadness or even pain for the harm you have caused others. This is especially likely to be true if those others don't accept your confession and forgive you. But that need not remove your sense of peace with God.

We are now ready to talk about the final step in overcoming legalism: conversion.

"But I was converted years ago," you say. "What do you mean, I need conversion?"

You probably were. But how often did Paul say he died? And what did he mean by "I die daily" (1 Cor. 15:31, KJV)? You will recall that in Romans 6 Paul used the death and resurrection of Jesus as an illustration of the Christian's death to self and his resurrection to a new way of life (see Rom. 6:3, 4). That's conversion. So if Paul said that he died every day, that means he was also raised to a new life every day. Or, to follow the illustration to its logical conclusion, Paul was *converted* every day.

I'd like to suggest that there are two aspects to conversion. The first is the one all sinners experience when they first come to Christ. Let's call this "general conversion." However, as we all know, God doesn't give us instant victory over all our character defects the moment we accept Him as our Saviour. Those defects take time to overcome. We have to be converted on each one, and on some of them—probably most of them—we will have to be converted many times, until the new way of life has become permanently fixed in our character. Since this aspect of conversion has to do with conversion on specific points—dealing with specific sins in our lives—let's call these repeated conversions "specific conversion." I believe that Paul was talking about specific conversion, not general conversion, when he wrote the part of Galatians 5 that we are examining in this chapter: "Those who belong to Christ Jesus have crucified the sinful nature with its passions and desires. Since we live by the Spirit, let us keep in step with the Spirit" (verses 24, 25).

You may wonder what those verses have to do with conversion. Quite a lot, actually. Notice that Galatians 5:24 speaks of the death of the sinful nature, and verses 16 and 25 speak of the new life in the Spirit. To live a "life in the Spirit" means to be converted. In verse 16 Paul said that the way to avoid living according to the old sinful nature is to live life in the Spirit, that is, to be converted.

Let's get specific about "life in the Spirit" and what it means to be converted.

In Romans 8:5 Paul said something similar to the verses we have just been discussing in Galatians: "Those who live according to the sinful nature," he said, "have their minds set on what that nature desires; but those who live in accordance with the Spirit have their minds set on what the Spirit desires."

I want you to notice one important point in Romans that Paul didn't mention in Galatians. He talked about having the mind "set." We can either set our minds on what our sinful nature desires, or we can set our minds on what the Spirit desires. Obviously, life in the Spirit means setting the mind on what the Spirit desires. The question is What does it mean to set the mind on what the Spirit desires? How do Christians do that?

It's not nearly as complicated as you might think. We've already talked about it. Do you remember those prayers I suggested you say? Let's look at them again:

1. God, show me if You see any way in which I'm a legalist.

2. Lord, if that's You talking, and if You really are trying to tell me I'm a legalist on this point, then keep bringing this thought back to me.

3. And Lord, if that really is You talking, then help me *want* to accept what You're telling me, even though right now I don't feel like accepting it.

To set the mind on what the Spirit desires means to choose God's way over what your sinful nature desires. And every time you say one of those prayers, you are choosing to put your mind on God's side. You are setting your mind on what the Spirit desires.

I must warn you, though, that it's not always easy to say those prayers. It's not always easy to choose God's way. It's not always easy to set your mind on the things of the Spirit. Here's how Paul described this problem: "For the sinful nature desires what is contrary to the Spirit, and the Spirit what is contrary to the sinful nature. They are in conflict with each other, so that you do not do what you want" (Gal. 5:18).*

Your old sinful nature isn't going to lie down and let itself be killed without a fight. You will discover that your desire to indulge in legalism will come back again and again. And sometimes it will seem *so right*. That's the deceptive thing about legalism. It *seems* right. And not only will it seem right; because it's a part of your sinful nature, you'll *want* to keep on doing it. You'll *want* to keep on being legalistic.

So how do you deal with that? Paul gave us a clue in verse 24: "Those who belong to Christ Jesus have crucified the sinful nature with its passions and desires."

What does it mean to crucify the sinful nature? Well, what does it mean to crucify anything? It means to take some boards and make a cross out of them, and then nail whatever it is you are going to crucify to that cross. Of course, you can't literally take your sinful nature out of your brain and nail it to a couple of boards in the shape of a cross. That's a metaphor. So what's the real meaning behind those words?

How would you like someone to lay you down on a cross, stretch out your hands, and drive nails through them, pinning your hands to the cross? And how would you like that same person to pin your feet to the cross with another nail? I suspect you wouldn't be too happy about that. In fact, I have no doubt that it would be the most difficult experience you ever went through!

That's what it means to crucify the sinful nature. It will be a painfully difficult experience—very likely the most painful experience you ever went through. That's why you need to stay close to the Spirit while you're doing it. That's why you need to keep saying those three prayers and any others you can think of like them. In fact, I'd like to give you a fourth prayer right now that will help you crucify that old sinful nature: "Lord, help me not to *want* to be a legalist." Each time you recognize a legalistic thought popping into your mind, each time you feel that old way of life pulling at your emotions, say that prayer. "Lord, help me not to want to be a legalist." "Take away my desire to be a legalist." "Change me so I no longer have the desire to be a legalist."

Saying those prayers will be the last thing you'll feel like doing at the moment when you have the greatest desire to indulge your old legalistic nature. Saying them will be a matter of pure choice, an exercise of your will. But if you say them, and keep saying them each time you are tempted to indulge your old legalistic nature, I guarantee you, it will work. God will make that change in your mind and heart, and you will discover legalism fading from your life—possibly more rapidly than you ever would have dreamed possible.

And here's some good news. You will be *so much happier* when you overcome your legalism. You'll sense the greatest freedom when you realize that you aren't responsible for everyone else's behavior in the church. You don't have to try to control them and feel frustrated or depressed when they refuse to cooperate.

And I have another bit of good news for you. The method for overcoming legalism that I just outlined works with any other sin that you may be trying to conquer.

---

*The Greek says "the flesh," not "the sinful nature." The words "sinful nature" are an interpretation by the NIV translators—albeit an accurate interpretation of what Paul meant, in my opinion.

Dealing With Legalists
Galatians 6

I had just arrived home from work and was sorting through the evening mail. Near the bottom of the stack I found the most recent issue of the *Adventist Review,* so I picked it up and began leafing through the pages. An article near the center of the magazine caught my attention enough that I started reading it. By the time I was into the third paragraph I couldn't put it down. I'd like to share several paragraphs with you.

"In the late 1970s my father, mother, sister, and I attended a Revelation Seminar given by an evangelist in Virginia. My father, mother, and sister accepted the Lord and desired to be baptized. I had not yet come to know the Lord, but there was pressure from my family and from the church to baptize a complete family, so I consented.

"After our baptism as a family, we fell into a routine of going to church for a while and then not going for a while. Needless to say, our lives and practices were not always in harmony with the standards of the church. During one of the out periods in our experience, the leading elders of the church came by to visit. I knew something was wrong when they refused to sit down or accept any hospitality. They said they were there on behalf of the church board.

"They said that the church board had voted to disconnect us from the church. They reasoned that our irregular attendance and other unrepresentative activities were a bad influence on other members. They said that we gave the community a wrong impression about Seventh-day Adventists. They did hold out the possibility that we could be accepted back into membership if we turned our lives around and became better Christians.

"I'll never forget that day or the intensity of my thoughts and feelings. Tears burned hot in my eyes. I ran to my room choking those tears back. Those men represented God to me; they were God's voice. Since they had rejected me, God must have rejected me too. I turned my anger on God, and I still remember the pain that I felt as I turned my back on Him" (May 14, 1992, p. 11).

The author went on to tell of the years of spiritual pain she endured. She is one of the fortunate few who, after receiving such treatment, reestablished a relationship with the church. The majority never do.

This author told her side of the story—the rejection by the church as she experienced it. I wish I could hear the other side of the story. It's possible that it would sound quite a bit different. Unfortunately, even if knowing the other side would moderate the apparent harshness in this particular case, the kind of thing this woman described happens all the time in conservative Christian denominations, including the Adventist Church. Therefore, I find it quite believable.

For now, let's assume that the incident happened more or less the way the author described it—that the elders who called on her family really were as callous as she felt them to be. It is a classic example of the human wreckage that legalists can leave in their wake. The leaders in this congregation appear to have been more concerned about the standards and the good name of the church than they were about the spiritual welfare of their wayward members.

I read the story to my wife while she was preparing our evening meal, and her immediate response was "How terrible! Why couldn't those elders have dealt with these people so as to save them instead of driving them away?"

That's a good question. Each of us needs to think about it, especially those of us who are leaders in God's church, who are called upon from time to time to deal with members who are not living in harmony with the teachings of the church and the Bible.

But I'd like to pose a different question: How could someone in the church who recognized the legalistic attitude of the elders have dealt with the elders themselves, who, sincere though they may have been, mishandled the situation so cruelly? That question brings us to the heart of what this chapter is about: dealing with legalists. And I'd like to suggest that that's what Paul spoke about in the first part of Galatians 6. He began by saying: "Brothers, if someone is caught in a sin, you who are spiritual should restore him gently" (verse 1).

Let's take a moment to review what we know of the history of the church in Galatia. Paul established the church in that region during an illness. He taught his new converts the gospel and left them rejoicing in their newfound faith. Unfortunately, after his departure a legalistically minded sect of Jewish Christians from Jerusalem infiltrated the church in Galatia, and they adopted a harsh attitude toward those who were not living up to the standards as they (the Jewish party) understood them. However, not everyone in the church accepted the teachings of the Jewish party. In fact, some members strongly resisted those teachings, to the point that the church became seriously divided. In due time war broke out, with each side openly criticizing and condemning the other.

This is the context of Paul's advice: "Brothers, if someone is caught in a sin, you who are spiritual should restore him gently."

The question is Who were the sinners Paul referred to? There are at least two possibilities. One is that the sinners were people whom the Jewish party and their Galatian sympathizers were trying to get to reform. Legalists are famous for treating harshly those whom they consider to be sinners, and perhaps Paul was encouraging them to be more gentle. Maybe he was saying, "You legalists, please deal gently with those who are struggling with bad language." "Please deal gently with the girls in the church who get pregnant out of wedlock." "Please deal gently with Gentiles who joined the church straight out of heathenism and still have a few bad habits to overcome."

However, I'd like you to think of this passage in a slightly different way—and this is the second way to think of the "sinners" Paul spoke about. Maybe he was asking the church to be more gentle with the legalists themselves! His harsh tone toward legalists earlier in Galatians seems to contradict that interpretation, but read the next two or three paragraphs before you give up that idea altogether.

In the last half of chapter 5 Paul contrasted the works of the flesh with the fruits of the Spirit, and in his list of "works of the flesh," he mentioned divisiveness and factions right alongside drunkenness and orgies. He warned the Galatian Christians to stop "biting and devouring each other" lest they destroy each other. And in the last verse of chapter 5 he said, "Let us not become conceited, provoking and envying each other."

Now, at the beginning of chapter 6, he said, "Brothers, if someone is caught in a sin . . ."

What sin? Who was sinning in Galatia? The people who were biting and devouring each other. The people who were creating divisions. The Jewish party and those whom they had won to their side. These were the people Paul said had indulged their sinful nature. These were the ones who needed restoration. And Paul said, "Brothers, if someone is caught in a sin, you who are spiritual should restore him *gently*."

It is impossible to say exactly who Paul had in mind when he spoke of the "sinners" in the church, but his advice to deal gently with them applies just as much to those who are guilty of legalism as to any other sin. That sounds strange, doesn't it, when we remember Paul's seemingly harsh advice in Galatians 4:30 to "get rid of the slave woman and her son"? However, legalism is a manifestation of the sinful nature, just like gluttony, drunkenness, and sexual immorality. If God has asked us to deal gently with people who are guilty of manifesting those aspects of the sinful nature that we call drunkenness and sexual immorality, why should we deal any differently with those who manifest aspects of the sinful nature that we call legalism?

Unfortunately, I must confess to you that the easiest attitude for non-legalists to take toward legalists is the very harshness they claim to see in legalists. The question is How can we deal gently with legalists when our first impulse is to be harsh with them?

Three things, I believe, will help.

First, we must remember that legalists have a perfect right to their views. We may not agree with their convictions, but we have an obligation to respect them. Even when they try to force their views onto others, we must respect those views. We should intervene in the forcing—and I will speak about that later—but even the fact that they are trying to force their views onto others does not give us a right to disrespect their convictions. We must not make fun of legalists or their views, regardless of how strange they may seem. As long as we disrespect the views of legalists, we remove ourselves from ever leading them to a clearer understanding of spiritual issues.

Second, we need to recognize that God loves legalists and helps them according to their understanding of right and wrong. This fact is illustrated by a family I knew several years ago that believed it was wrong to wear clothes made from two kinds of fiber (see Lev. 19:19). When they went to the department store to buy clothes for the children, they explained to the clerk that they were looking for garments that were made of 100 percent cotton. All-cotton garments were hard to find back then, yet here was a family looking for all-cotton clothing from the top of the head to the soles of the feet for several boys and girls of varying sizes! The clerk searched and searched, and finally found garments for each child that were made entirely of cotton. Pants, shirts, skirts—everything was cotton.

There was a problem, though. The all-cotton clothes cost about three times as much as the garments that were made of blended fibers. Apparently the demand for all-cotton garments was so small that the manufacturer had to keep the price high in order to make a profit.

The father explained to the clerk the family's religious beliefs and asked if, under the circumstances, the store might be willing to sell the family the cotton clothes at the same price as clothing made from blended fibers. The clerk excused himself. A few moments later he returned and said that his supervisor had granted the family's request.

You can imagine the father's joy when he told me the story a few days later. "Look how the Lord provided!" he exclaimed. "It always pays to obey what the Bible says."

You and I smile at that story. We shake our heads and think, *Really, now, did God stoop to supporting people in that kind of nonsense?*

And I say yes. Absolutely! I believe that God honors everyone's honest convictions. I believe each of us has beliefs that make Him smile. I doubt there's a person alive who doesn't do things now and then that cause Him and the angels to chuckle—or to weep. Does that mean He helps us only when our ideas and our behavior make sense to *Him?* Of course not! Does a parent withhold a simple request from a child just because the parent thinks the request is foolish? Some parents may, but I can assure you they are not the best parents. As long as it's affordable and it doesn't hurt anyone, the best parents give their children what they ask for, regardless of what the parents may think of it.

So the second principle to keep in mind as we rub shoulders with legalists is that God loves them and works with them within their perception of what is right and wrong.

The third thing to keep in mind about legalists is that they are utterly sincere. I have yet to meet legalists whose purpose in life was to destroy the church. They want to help the church. They want to help their families.

Several years ago, when I was a pastor in Texas, I had a church member who was known for his legalistic attitude. This man came to see me in my office one day. He wanted to talk about his children. The children were young enough that they were still conforming to their father's wishes, but I feared that his harsh, judgmental spirit would in due time drive them away from their spiritual roots and away from the church. Yet this dear man wept as he shared with me his deep concern for his children. He wasn't trying to drive them from the church. Nothing was closer to his heart than those children, and he desperately wanted to see them saved.

Legalists are utterly sincere, and no one can minister redemptively to their needs who is unable to see beneath their harsh exterior this deep longing for the whole church to be right with God.

To minister effectively to legalists, then, we must respect their views, even though we disagree with them. We must recognize that God loves them and works with them on their terms, not ours. And we must understand that their desire to see the church prosper is just as deep as ours. If we can approach legalists in this way, we will be much more likely to follow Paul's advice and deal with them gently.

Paul mentioned an extremely important quality about those who are called upon to deal with sinners in the church, including those guilty of the sin of legalism. He said that they must be spiritual. "If someone is caught in a sin," he said, "you who are *spiritual* should restore him gently." To be spiritual means to have a close relationship with Jesus. It means to have certain gifts of the Spirit, such as faith, wisdom, and discernment. It's extremely important that the church appoint only the most spiritual people to deal with those who are creating factions and divisions in the congregation. In most cases, this will be the elders, who were appointed to that position because of their qualifications for spiritual leadership.

In the second half of verse 1 Paul said something else that is important: "But watch yourself, or you also may be tempted."

Those whom the church asks to deal with sin must be careful lest the very sin they are trying to correct in others rubs off on them. And nowhere is this danger greater than in our dealings with legalists. Legalists have the unique ability to arouse in the rest of us the same harshness that we condemn in them. This happens because legalists arouse feelings of anger in us, which leads to harshness. Those of us who are not legalists—or think we aren't—tend to become angry with legalists for two reasons. First, we become angry when they try to force their views on us. And second, we become angry when their harsh, judgmental spirit injures weaker Christians.

That's why legalism can wreak such havoc in a church. It's not just the legalists' anger that gets out of control. Often those who are trying to deal with legalists become just as angry. The legalists get mad at the nonlegalists, and the nonlegalists get mad at the legalists. Soon the whole church is in an uproar.

Let's examine verses 3-5 in light of the problem of legalism that Paul was dealing with in Galatia. Paul said, "If anyone thinks he is something when he is nothing, he deceives himself. Each one should test his own actions. Then he can take pride in himself, without comparing himself to somebody else, for each one should carry his own load." This is extremely important advice for those of us who have to deal with legalists.

I recently read an extremely harsh, judgmental letter that a certain man wrote to some friends criticizing a group of people he thought were legalistic. It was obvious that this man thought quite highly of his own spiritual qualifications. Yet his letter was filled with accusations and subtle remarks about the supposed narrow-mindedness of his opponents. In my opinion, this man should have judged himself before he judged those whom he was accusing. He should have tested his own words and actions before he tested theirs (see Matt. 7:1-5). Those who speak derisively of legalists are actually comparing themselves with the legalists and saying, "God, I thank You I'm not like those legalists" (see Luke 18:11). It's so easy for nonlegalists to think they are something when they are nothing!

I'd like now to call your attention to an apparent contradiction I referred to earlier between what I've said so far in this chapter and what I have said in previous chapters. Throughout most of this book I have taken quite a hard line toward legalists. I did that because Paul did. In Galatians 3:1 he said, "You foolish Galatians! Who has bewitched you?" In chapter 4, verse 17 he said, "Those people are zealous to win you over, but for no good. What they want is to alienate you from us, so that you may be zealous for them." Later in chapter 4 he said, "Get rid of the slave woman and her son" (verse 30). And in chapter 5 he said, "You who are trying to be justified by law have been alienated from Christ; you have fallen away from grace" (verse 4). Finally, he said, "As for those agitators, I wish they would go the whole way and emasculate [castrate] themselves!" (verse 12).

There can be no doubt that throughout most of his letter to the Galatians, Paul opposed legalists with some of the strongest language anywhere in his writings. How, then, could he advise taking such a gentle attitude toward them in the first few verses of chapter 6? At first glance, this is one of the best reasons for supposing that the sinners Paul spoke about in verse 1 were *not* the legalists in the Galatian congregations. It would be easy to suppose his call for gentleness applied to those whom the legalists were persecuting, not to the legalists themselves. I'm sure everyone will agree that we should deal gently with those whom legalists persecute. But I believe Paul's appeal for gentle treatment applies equally to our dealings with legalists, because legalism is a sin—a manifestation of the sinful nature—just as much as adultery.

So how do we do both? How do we "get rid of" legalists and at the same time treat them gently?

To begin with, I don't think "get rid of" means to be harsh or callous. If those are the qualities we do not like in the legalists, we certainly should not use them against them, much as we may be tempted to. I prefer the word "firm." Gentle and harsh are opposites, like hot and cold or wet and dry. But gentle and firm go well together. It is possible to treat a person both firmly and gently. I believe that "firm" is the word we need to think of when we read Paul's advice to "get rid of the slave woman and her son."

In chapter 15 of this book I described in some detail three attitudes that characterize legalists. Let's discuss how to deal both firmly and gently with each of these attitudes.

The first one is "attitudes about sin and salvation." Surely we shouldn't have a problem dealing gently with someone when we're talking about salvation! The trouble comes when legalists express ideas about salvation that contradict Scripture, such as an exclusively behavioral definition of sin. I believe we have a responsibility to respond to ideas that will lead people to a false understanding of the gospel. We deal with this problem firmly by expressing our understanding of Scripture with conviction. We deal with it gently by showing respect for the views of the legalists, by recognizing that they have as much of a right to their views as you and I do to ours. We often call this "pluralism"—a word that means tolerance of a variety of ideas.

"But the legalists in my church get angry with me when I talk about pluralism," you say. "They accuse me of apostasy when I contradict their views."

That happens in all too many cases. When it does, you are dealing with a control issue, which is the third attitude I will discuss. For now, let's stick with pluralism.

Pluralism does not mean that all ideas are right. It means that we respect the right of others within the church to hold views that differ from ours. Some teachings cannot be tolerated, of course. I don't know of a church in the land that would tolerate the idea that it is appropriate for Christians to abuse children sexually. Anyone who taught that in a Sabbath school class or a Sunday school class ought to certainly be removed from his or her position and reprimanded severely.

However, every church also has teachings on which there are a variety of opinions, and it is possible to hold any of the views and still be a member. Even teachings that are nonnegotiable may have ramifications that are. For example, Seventh-day Adventists, along with most other Christians, accept the teaching of salvation by grace alone through faith. If you were to stand up in a Seventh-day Adventist pulpit and teach that people are saved by works, you would rightly be denied access to the pulpit again. But subtle variations exist within that teaching that are subject to a variety of interpretations, and these we need to tolerate and respect, even when we disagree strongly. The same, I believe, is true of differences of opinion about the divine-human nature of Christ, lifestyle standards, styles of worship, various types of music, etc.

We may express strong disagreement with legalists, but we must always do it with respect. That's how we deal with them *both* firmly *and* gently. And that's also pluralism. When we learn to treat differences of opinion that way, in many cases that will be the end of the problem. And when it is, who really was at fault—you and I, or the person we thought was a legalist?

The second attitude I mentioned in chapter 15 that is characteristic of many legalists is a rigid, overly literal interpretation of Scripture—using the Bible as a rulebook, often in ways that seem ridiculously extreme to everyone else. An example of this is the idea that Deuteronomy 22:5 means women shouldn't wear pants or that Leviticus 19:27 means men shouldn't trim the corners of their beards.

How do we deal both firmly and gently with legalists on that?

If they aren't trying to push their views onto others, the firmly part shouldn't be much of a problem. We can all agree, I'm sure, that the issue is not orthodoxy. You probably wouldn't even have to remove a teacher who was advocating these ideas in a Sabbath school or Sunday school class. In most cases, the problem would take care of itself within a couple of weeks when 90 percent of the members of the class decided to go somewhere else.

As long as legalists are willing to hold their views privately, our approach should be more gentle than firm. We should respect their views, odd though they may seem to us. We should rejoice with them when God answers their prayers. We should avoid ridiculing their views either in public or in private.

The third attitude that characterizes many legalists is the tough one: control. How can we deal both gently and firmly with legalists who are trying to control other people and perhaps the entire church? How can we deal gently with people who are criticizing and condemning the church over a "moral issue" that the rest of us don't think has anything to do with morality?

The first thing to keep in mind is that while the word "gently" means respecting the views of legalists, it does not mean caving in to them, doing things their way to avoid a fight. It does not mean being nice, refusing to confront. It does not mean allowing legalists to harass people unimpeded. It does not mean tolerating their unacceptable behavior.

Let's discuss this matter of control on two levels: personal and corporate. First, how can a Christian deal with legalists who are trying to control him or her personally, and second, how can a church deal with legalists who are trying to control the entire congregation?

On the personal level, remember that there are two kinds of legalists: the gentle kind and the harsh kind. If a gentle legalist comes up to you with a smile and speaks softly about something in your way of life that he or she thinks is wrong, don't get angry. Move the issue away from what you're doing to a philosophical discussion of the issue itself. Say something like, "You know, while I disagree with you on this question, I respect your right to believe as you do. What Bible evidence do you have for your views?" Most legalists will jump at the chance to answer that question. Whereupon you will have shifted the discussion from your personal practice to what the Bible says about your practice. Instead of escalating the argument, you've defused it. You've handled it gently.

Suppose that after presenting his Bible evidence the legalist asks you for yours. Even if you have a good answer, sharing it right then would probably get the two of you into an argument that could easily lead straight back to your behavior. Just smile and say, "Let's talk about my Bible evidence next time." If you aren't sure how to explain your point of view from the Bible, admit it. You might say, "I'm not sure what the Bible says about that. I guess I'll have to go home and study this question some more."

That's one way to defuse the gentle legalist who approaches you with a smile. There are many other ways.

It's a different matter when the legalist criticizes you harshly for your way of life. Some people will get angry at the harsh legalist, storm out of the church, and never return. Anyone who does that has fallen straight into the legalist's trap.

There's a much better way. It begins with keeping pluralism in mind. You must insist that the legalist respect your views as much as you respect his or hers. This means *setting a limit* on what you will allow a legalist to say to you. I recommend that you smile and say something like this: "Thank you for your interest in my spiritual well-being. However, I have strong personal convictions about this matter, and I'll appreciate your not speaking to me about it again."

The gentle part of this answer is thanking the person with a smile for showing interest in your well-being. You have affirmed his or her sincere desire to help you. The firm part is *setting a limit* on what you will allow that person to say to you. That's how you "get rid of the slave woman and her son" gently.

This approach will stop 95 percent of the harsh legalists in their tracks. Many of them will feel that they've done their Christian duty by talking to you, and you'll never hear from them again. I'm convinced that most people are decent enough to respect a firmly drawn line. If you are attacked again by the same person, say the same thing calmly, but with a neutral expression on your face this time instead of a smile. The third time you should say, "We've discussed this before, and I've told you what I expect from you." Then walk away.

In a rare case when the person still keeps attacking you, follow Matthew 18:15-20. You've already spoken to this person several times between the two of you alone. Now it's time to ask the pastor or an elder to visit him or her with you. If that doesn't settle the problem, ask the church board to help.

Notice that at no time is it necessary, in any of these steps, to lose your temper. This is crucial. As long as you speak respectfully to the other person, in a controlled tone of voice, you are being both gentle and firm.

What can a church do when one or more legalists are trying to impose their views on the entire congregation? This problem is the closest to what Paul was dealing with in Galatia, and it is best handled by the church's leadership. And again it should be handled gently. I've seen miracles come out of handling a church conflict with a delicate touch, a bit of humor, and a relaxed attitude on the part of the pastor and other leaders.

One way to handle a church conflict gently is to talk to everyone involved. The elders and the pastor can visit individually with the people on both sides, sort of on a fact-finding mission. They should sincerely ask for each person's point of view, listen, treat everyone with respect, and avoid saying a whole lot. A solution may emerge from these conversations that will satisfy everyone.

If this doesn't work, it may be necessary to call a meeting of both sides. Again, it's a good idea to keep the discussion in a fact-finding mode. Write the facts as each side understands them on a board, and see if there isn't some middle ground, a compromise that can be worked out, that everyone can buy into. If the conflict is quite strong, it might be a good idea to invite an outside person—perhaps a pastor from another church whom everyone trusts—to lead out in the discussion. An extremely bitter church split is best handled by someone who is trained in the skills of conflict resolution. This will cost some money, but it may be the only way to save the church.

And through it all, those who are trying to settle the problem down must remember that firmness does not mean rudeness or disrespect. It means drawing a line. The majority in the church will have to tell the legalists that the subject they are insisting on will not be discussed any further, and anyone who insists on bringing it up again will be asked to drop the matter immediately. Most people will go along with this request.

One other point in conclusion. It's vital to remember that Paul's advice in Galatians 6 isn't just about settling personal differences and church fights. Paul said, "When someone is caught in a sin, you who are spiritual should *restore* him gently." Paul's whole point was restoration. His remarks in Galatians 5 make it utterly clear that legalism is a sin, which means that the church should try to restore legalists. And that means helping them come to the place that they are no longer legalistic. That's difficult to do, because of all sinners, legalists are least likely to recognize their own problems. They are sure that they are right and everyone else is wrong.

Restoring legalists to a truly Christian way of life is one of the most difficult challenges facing Christian leaders. It requires a great deal of prayer. I believe our most earnest prayers should be for ourselves, that the Lord will work in each of us the changes that we need in order that we can do for them what they need.

This brings us to the end of our study of Galatians, with the exception of a few concluding remarks that Paul used, which we need to examine. In some cases these concluding remarks are related to the rest of the book and in some cases they are not. I have classed all of them as concluding remarks because even those that are related to what Paul said earlier appear to come after he wrapped up his main argument.

Let's review these concluding remarks briefly.

The first one obviously has nothing to do with Paul's theology of salvation or the problem of the Jewish party and legalism. Paul said, "Anyone who receives instruction in the word must share all good things with his instructor" (verse 6). Even today we sometimes debate on church boards whether the organist, the choir director, and the church treasurer should volunteer their time or be paid for their services. Apparently a similar question came up in the Galatian congregations with respect to remunerating those who were teachers. Paul said, "Pay them."

Next we come to a fairly long passage that is related to what Paul said earlier, but because it is separated from his earlier remarks by this bit of advice to pay Christian teachers, it seems likely that it is another of his concluding remarks. "Do not be deceived: God cannot be mocked. A man reaps what he sows. The one who sows to please his sinful nature, from that nature will reap destruction; the one who sows to please the Spirit, from the Spirit will reap eternal life. Let us not become weary in doing good, for at the proper time we will reap a harvest if we do not give up. Therefore, as we have opportunity, let us do good to all people, especially to those who belong to the family of believers" (verses 7-10).

I'd like to call attention to a couple of points. First, you may not have realized it, but the familiar proverb "You reap what you sow" comes from this passage in Galatians. Paul's point is that any sin Christians do not bring under control will control them and eventually destroy them. Second, his plea that the Galatians "do good to all people, especially to those who belong to the family of believers" may have been a final appeal to those in the church who were quarrelling to start treating each other kindly.

"See what large letters I use as I write to you with my own hand!" Paul said in verse 11. In two or three places throughout his letters it is evident that Paul wrote by dictating to a scribe (see, for example, Rom. 16:22).

However, here he called attention to his own handwriting at the end (see also 2 Thess. 3:17). This was probably his way of authenticating the letter as his own, the way we do when we sign our name at the end of our letters. There were probably plenty of false apostles around who would have been more than glad to whip out a letter in Paul's name and circulate it among the churches. Paul's handwritten note at the end made that impossible.

Notice that Paul called attention to the fact that his handwriting was much larger than the scribe's. This may have been because of his poor eyesight (see Gal. 4:15). If he had had better eyesight, he might have written all of his Epistles himself.

Poor Paul. He felt so upset with the Jewish party that he had to make one final appeal for the Galatian Christians to pay no attention to them: "Those who want to make a good impression outwardly are trying to compel you to be circumcised. The only reason they do this is to avoid being persecuted for the cross of Christ. Not even those who are circumcised obey the law, yet they want you to be circumcised that they may boast about your flesh" (verses 12, 13).

Probably the most significant question this passage raises is Why did Paul say that the Jewish party's motive in getting the Gentile Christians in Galatia to be circumcised was to "avoid being persecuted for the cross of Christ" themselves? Who was persecuting the Jewish party, and how would getting the Gentile believers circumcised spare them that persecution? The persecution probably came from non-Christian Jews who accused the Christian Jews of destroying the faith of their fathers. Paul suggested that the Jewish party's insistence on Gentile Christians submitting to circumcision was motivated, in part at least, by their desire to respond to this criticism.

A whole chapter could be written about Paul's next sentence. Certainly many sermons have been preached on it. "May I never boast," he said, "except in the cross of our Lord Jesus Christ, through which the world has been crucified to me, and I to the world" (verse 14). Paul probably made this remark to contrast his motive for preaching with the motive of the Jewish party. That Paul had to write such a forceful letter to the Galatian Christians suggests that the Jewish party had won many converts among them, and apparently the Jewish party was boasting about their huge success (see Gal. 4:17). Paul said, "I don't want to boast about anything except the cross of Jesus."

"Neither circumcision nor uncircumcision means anything," he continued. "What counts is a new creation" (verse 15). In other words, it's not the externals of religion that count, but the condition of the heart. And then he added, "Peace and mercy to all who follow this rule, even to the Israel of God" (verse 16).

The expression "Israel of God" seems to be a reference to all the Christians in Galatia, both Jews and Gentiles. Some interpreters of Galatians have suggested that by his use of the word "Israel" Paul was singling out the Jewish Christians for a special blessing. However, that would have contradicted his words in Galatians 3:28 that in Christ "there is neither Jew nor Greek." It is more consistent with his line of reasoning in Galatians to interpret the word "Israel" symbolically. All Christians have inherited the promise of righteousness by faith that God made to Abraham (see Gal. 3:29), and therefore all Christians, both Jews and Gentiles, are the new Israel.

"Finally, let no one cause me trouble," Paul said next, "for I bear on my body the marks of Jesus" (verse 17). With this comment he seems to have brought his argument in Galatians full circle. His first remark in Galatians, and indeed his line of reasoning throughout the entire first chapter, was a defense of his apostleship. Now at the end he came back to that theme. By "marks of Jesus" "on my body," he meant the scars from the beatings and other forms of persecution he had endured while preaching the gospel. He said, in effect, "Tell the Jewish party to stop making trouble over my apostleship. The marks of that persecution, which I carry on my body, are the best evidence that I am a genuine apostle."

At the beginning of our study we noticed that Paul opened with a greeting that was similar in many respects to the "Dear John" with which we begin our letters today. In the same way, he also said, "Sincerely, Paul." He didn't use those exact words, of course. That's not how they did it back then. Here's what he said: "The grace of our Lord Jesus Christ be with your spirit, brothers. Amen" (verse 18). We sometimes close our letters on a similar Christian note by saying things like "Yours in Christ" or "Yours in His service." I like what a friend of mine often says: "Yours and His."

Verse 18 seems like a fitting conclusion to a letter in which Paul has spoken so vigorously and so frankly. It's also a fitting conclusion to this book: "The grace of our Lord Jesus Christ be with your spirit, brothers. Amen."